Troublesome Bible Passages

Lessons from 23 Familiar Texts

Contents

From the Editor

"What is your favorite Bible passage?" This question brought many responses from United Methodists across the nation. That response led us to produce a study book containing many of the favorite Bible passages that people suggested.

Then some of our readers reported that we had failed to include "my favorite Bible passage." Consequently, a second volume was produced for study with a new set of favorites of our audience. We are sure that there are still many Bible-reading Christians who would like to have their favorite Scripture passage or verse included in a future study book. We are not sure about that at this moment, but we can certainly hope for it with them. Nonetheless, it is indeed very encouraging and gratifying to know of such interest among United Methodists.

During the time of developing *Favorite Bible Passages*, another concern was brought to our attention regarding some Scripture passages that troubled many dedicated and devoted Christians. These Scripture passages appear to be troublesome in their theological implications, in their use of difficult language or uncommon imagery, or in their application to life in today's world. Some passages seem to be contradictory to other passages in the Bible ascribed to the same person as the source of those statements.

Are there contradictions in God's Word? Did Jesus give some opposing messages? Was Paul guilty of the same when writing to the churches? The first answer is no. The second answer is that to some it appears to be so. We will deal with the *appearance* aspect of the Bible passages and will seek to find the transforming message that each selected verse or passage has for us, the Bible being God's Word for us in our time and world.

The word *antinomy* may help us here. The *American Heritage Dictionary of the English Language* (Third Edition) defines it as "1. Contradiction or opposition, especially between two laws or rules. 2. A contradiction between principles or conclusions that seem equally necessary and reasonable; a paradox." Was Jesus Christ fully divine or fully human? There is an apparent contradiction here, but both ideas bear the truth. Did Jesus come bearing peace or a sword? Both ideas bear the truth.

Some troublesome passages deal with issues of social and economic justice—the parable of the laborers in the vineyard, for example, in which the laborers who came to work late in the day were paid the same wages as the ones who worked all day. How is this justifiable? What is the transforming message here?

Is sinning a matter of choice, or is it something we are born to do as human beings? What is the story of Adam and Eve teaching us? Why do innocent and God-fearing people suffer? What sins did Job commit to deserve one tragedy after another? What are the theological implications in these stories for us? What is the transforming message here?

Some troublesome passages are extremely hard to follow through on or apply in our daily life. Peter asked Jesus, "How often [how many times] should I forgive? As many as seven times?" (Matthew 18:21). How helpful is Jesus' answer ("seventy-seven times") for the person who keeps sinning against you? What is the transforming message here?

The Scripture passages that have been selected for study in this book have the potential to help us grow toward faith and discipleship. They seem to challenge the status quo of personal value systems and of inadequate notions of what it means to be faithful as Christians today. These passages are more or less familiar to Christians and reflect a steadfast movement of God's plans for humanity recorded in the Holy Bible from Genesis to Revelation.

Our prayer is that this study will inculcate the enthusiasm and seriousness that we all need to have in exploring God's Word for the good news that is redeeming and transforming for us personally and for all God's children in God's household.

Victor J. Jacobs
Editor, TROUBLESOME BIBLE PASSAGES

1

Is All This Sinning Really Necessary?

Genesis 3:1-24

But the LORD God called to the man, and said to him, "Where are you?" He said, "I heard the sound of you in the garden, and I was afraid, because I was naked; and I hid myself."

Genesis 3:9-10

WORDS FOR BIBLE TIMES

The story of Adam and Eve in the garden is the story of human sin and its consequence. The first humans, representative of us all, are told that they can eat of the fruit of any tree except one. But the serpent, symbolizing a Tempter outside ourselves, points out that this is the very fruit that will open their eyes and make them like God, knowing good and evil. It was tasty, attractive, and would make them wise. So, out of their desire to be powerful and all-knowing like God, they ate, became aware of their vulnerability, and tried to cover themselves up.

Their newfound knowledge made them conscious that they had disobeyed God, so they hid in the bushes. But God sought them out, calling, "Where are you?" When confronted with their sin, the man blamed the woman and the woman accused the serpent. In punishment for this three-way conspiracy, the serpent was condemned to slither in the dust, the woman was assigned the pain of childbearing and the indignity of subservience to men, and the man had to earn his liv-

ing by the sweat of his brow. Their destiny would be to die
and return to the dust from whence they had come.

This first couple were named Adam, or Human, and Eve,
meaning Life or mother of all living. In spite of their sin, God
cared for them by making garments from animal skins to
clothe them. But because of their ambition to become like
God, know good and evil, and live forever, they were driven
out of the comfortable life of the garden never to return.

WORDS FOR OUR TIME

This story of Adam and Eve troubles many of us because it
suggests that sin is inherited, and it troubles all of us because
it confronts us with our own sinful tendencies. Many do not
believe we should blame our self-centeredness and desire to
play God on our ancestors, on woman as temptress, or on man
or the Devil symbolized as serpent. But we all are confronted
in the story with our own misuse of the freedom and opportunity God has given us. The story of Adam and Eve forces us
to think about the origins of sin, and to face our prideful, self-
serving tendencies.

The story reveals the essence of human sin as the desire for
unlimited freedom without responsibility. We want to do as
we please without regard for the purposes of God or the
effects on others. This self-centered grasping for power and
control always gets us into trouble. Rather than trusting God's
guidance, we want to do things our way. When we refuse to
recognize the rule of God over our lives, the free, spontaneous
relationship we have had with one another is destroyed, the
order of society is upset, and we are separated from God, one
another, and our own best selves.

Like Adam and Eve, we protest that this is not our fault.
We shift the blame to causes outside ourselves—our instincts,
our upbringing, our circumstances, our spouses or friends—
even God. We think that if we can protest our innocence we
can avoid the effects of our misdeeds.

These self-serving acts do have consequences, however.
The curse on the serpent represents the effects of sin on
the natural world—cruelty and suffering in the animal
kingdom, pollution and destruction of the environment,

6

disease and decay that destroy the beauty and bounty of the earth.

The subordination of some persons to others was taken for granted in the hierarchical, patriarchal society of the ancient world, and this story attributes its source to our desire to play God. This male-dominated social order was challenged by Jesus through his respectful, caring treatment of women, as well as by Paul, who said, "There is no longer male and female; for all of you are one in Christ Jesus" (Galatians 3:28).

While marriage and children are part of God's good plan (Genesis 1:27-28), this story traces the pain and struggles of parenthood to human disobedience. Likewise, God intended work to be pleasant and creative (Genesis 1:28-29; 2:15), but selfishness has made life a burden and turned work into back-breaking toil—whether tilling the soil, running a monotonous machine, or experiencing the frustration and boredom of a routine job. Whenever we put our benefit ahead of God and the well-being of others, the result is damage to others, ourselves, and the God who hurts with all who suffer.

Original sin does not mean that we become evil simply by being born. Rather, we share with Adam and Eve a common desire to be Number One, to pretend to be all-wise, and to serve ourselves at the expense of all around us. Sin is not inherited genetically. Rather, human society passes on these tendencies through the way children are raised; the way wrong choices get repeated; and the way pride, ambition, and selfishness are rewarded materially. We are conditioned by our surroundings to repeat the mistakes of the first parents. Like them, we are given our opportunity; we are made in the image of God. But we abuse this freedom, deny God's intentions for us, and bring calamity and suffering onto ourselves. Thus the sinful cycle repeats itself over and over again.

God does not give up on us, however. Even when we selfishly disobey and cause trouble for ourselves and others, God still loves us. This is symbolized by the garments God made to shield the couple from the elements. While God's judgment is firm and will not excuse us when we violate the moral law, God's nature is also to forgive and to have mercy. No matter how we may try to escape, God is always with us.

"Where can I go from your spirit?
    Or where can I flee from your presence?
If I ascend to heaven, you are there;
    if I make my bed in Sheol, you are there.
If I take the wings of the morning
    and settle at the farthest limits of the sea,
even there your hand shall lead me"
                        (Psalm 139:7-10).

WORDS FOR MY LIFE

As seniors in high school, Judy and Don had slipped once and Judy had become pregnant. When this became known, she was judged and rejected by her parents. Both had to drop out of school, and life became miserable for everyone. They were not ready for marriage, but neither adoption nor abortion were options; so they were forced into it. Emotionally immature and financially unstable, their early marriage was rocky, and their children felt much stress. They had abused their freedom, and now both they and their children and parents were paying the price.

But God did not forsake them. Through facing shame and ostracism, they sought God's forgiveness and guidance. They confessed their moral lapse, had a church wedding, and began their marriage with regular church attendance and family prayer. Like Adam and Eve, they had eaten the forbidden fruit by doing things their way; but having acknowledged their sin, they found pardon and new life in God's love.

Each of us knows that we have violated God's commands and purposes for our life. We may try to blame parents for the way they raised us, conditions that made us susceptible to temptation, other persons who provoked us, Adam and Eve from whom we inherited sinful desires, the Devil who made us do it, or God who created us and thrust us into this evil, stressful life. But in our hearts we know that we are the ones responsible. Our sin is the tendency to make ourselves and our desires—rather than God—the center of our life. It is not necessarily the specific behavior that is sinful but rather the inner attitude and motivation: We are serving and worshiping ourselves rather than the God who made us.

We all grow up self-centered because of the emphasis in our culture on getting our needs met first. But we need not remain in this state. The God who asked Adam and Eve, "Where are you?" is searching for us in the bushes as well. God is pained because we seek so deliberately and foolishly to harm ourselves and others by not doing the divine will.

But whatever we do we cannot escape the circle of God's love. The God who cared for the first parents enough to make them garments of skins also loves us enough to clothe us in the divine grace offered in Christ. The only way to cease our sinning is to accept God's forgiveness and strength to resist temptation. On our own we yield too readily to the wiles of the Tempter who tells us, "Never mind what God says; do it my way." But Jesus opens a way to repent of our self-serving, turn back to God, and return to faithful living.

Like Adam and Eve, we can never return to a paradise free from struggle, pain, and temptation. But thanks to the grace of Christ, we can receive strength sufficient for every test. God's Spirit is always with us. "For . . . neither death, nor life, nor angels, nor rulers, nor things present, nor things to come, nor powers, nor height, nor depth, nor anything else in all creation, will be able to separate us from the love of God in Christ Jesus our Lord" (Romans 8:38-39).

2

Absolute Commitment
Genesis 22:1-19

Says the LORD: Because you have done this, and have not withheld your son, your only son, I will indeed bless you.

Genesis 22:16-17

WORDS FOR BIBLE TIMES

Abram (later Abraham) has already proved himself to be a person of faith. Responding to God's call to "Go from your country and your kindred . . . to the land that I will show you" (Genesis 12:1), he has left Haran and gone to dwell in the land of Canaan. When God promises that he and Sarah, even in their old age, will become the parents of a people as numerous as the stars in the sky, "he believed the LORD; and the LORD reckoned it to him as righteousness" (15:6). No wonder that Paul points to him as a model of faith: "No distrust made him waver concerning the promise of God, but he grew strong in his faith as he gave glory to God, being fully convinced that God was able to do what he had promised" (Romans 4:20-21).

But his greatest test is yet to come. God calls Abraham's name, and he responds, "Here I am," a sign that he is ready to do God's bidding. God tells him to take "your only son Isaac, whom you love," and present him as a burnt offering. So he calls Isaac, gathers the wood, makes the journey, and takes out his knife. Little Isaac, knowing that an animal is usually used in such circumstances, asks in all innocence, "Where is the lamb?" His father, no doubt heart-broken at what is about to occur, but still acting in faith and obedience, replies, "God . . . will provide."

With the altar built, the fire laid, and Isaac bound and placed atop the wood, Abraham prepares to strike the fatal blow. Then God's angel calls a second time, and Abraham—still at God's service—once again responds, "Here I am." Then come these welcome words: "Do not lay your hand on the boy or do anything to him; for now I know that you fear God, since you have not withheld your son, your only son, from me." Abraham looks up, sees a ram in the thicket, offers it in place of his son, and names the place "The LORD will provide." For his faithfulness, God confers a blessing on Abraham. His descendants will be numerous, "and by your offspring shall all the nations of the earth gain blessing . . . , because you have obeyed my voice."

WORDS FOR OUR TIME

This story troubles us because it seems to suggest that God would demand a child's murder to test our faith. But a closer look reveals that this experience of Abraham put an end to infant sacrifice in ancient times when the firstborn belonged to God—at least for the Hebrew people. In the Old Testament, animal sacrifice early replaced the human sacrifice practiced by Israel's neighbors as a means of atoning for sin. God would not require parents to end the life of a child near and dear to them.

This is being written soon after the tragedy in Waco, Texas, where David Koresh took his followers, including many children, to a fiery death. The Branch Davidians seem to have believed that this sacrifice of human life was God's will, but the story of Abraham and Isaac disputes that conclusion. God spared Isaac because God, who had worked a miracle to bring Isaac into the world, wanted him to continue the line begun by Abraham and Sarah. And God wants us to raise our children to love and serve God, not to harm them physically, emotionally, or spiritually.

Furthermore, the Bible teaches us that since Jesus by his death atoned for all sin, even animal sacrifice is obsolete. "Unlike the other high priests, he has no need to offer sacrifices day after day, first for his own sins, and then for those of the people; this he did once for all when he offered himself" (Hebrews 7:27).

Of course, Jesus does call his followers to sacrifice—to "deny themselves and take up their cross and follow me" (Mark 8:34). This is a call for willing surrender to serve Christ—to give our time, energy, and abilities to fulfill the purposes for which he came—teaching God's love; healing body, mind, and spirit; and increasing love and justice in all human relationships. Christian sacrifice is self-motivated and self-giving (not necessarily in blood) for the well-being of others and the glory of God. This is a far cry from killing other living beings to satisfy legal requirements of a jealous god.

Abraham was put to the test as he faced the tension between loyalty to family and obedience to God. He thought that contrary things were being demanded of him, and only at the end did he experience a loving God showing him that serving God and caring for loved ones were not in conflict. Jesus summarized the commandments as loving God fully and one's neighbor as oneself (Matthew 22:37-39). First John says, "Those who do not love a brother or sister whom they have seen, cannot love God whom they have not seen" (1 John 4:20). We show our loyalty to God *by* loving and serving the welfare of our families. The two injunctions do not conflict, but rather are in accord.

Of course, sometimes what seems best for our families may be different from what we feel God wants us to do. We may be led to give up a morally questionable job, take a challenging but low-paying position, move to a new area, live more simply to conserve natural resources, or take a controversial stand on an ethical issue. Any of these choices that we make in seeking to be faithful to God may bring sacrifices that affect our families. But if they know we love them, and at the same time are trying to be faithful to the good and the just, and if they trust us to put Christian values ahead of things, they will know they are better off with a life of integrity than with prosperity and material abundance.

Jesus spoke to this tension when, in the presence of his own earthly family, he said, "Whoever does the will of my Father in heaven is my brother and sister and mother"

(Matthew 12:50). By being faithful to what Jesus wants of us, we demonstrate our loyalty to him, and this is in the best interest of our families in the long run.

WORDS FOR MY LIFE

Myung-Ho Kim is a second generation Korean-American teenager whose Christian parents came to this country seeking a better life. They have high hopes for him and push him hard to do well in school, attend church, obey authority, and observe traditional Korean customs. Myung-Ho, however, has learned modern American ways from his school friends and wants to be free to date, make his own choices, and follow teenage customs in dress, language, and lifestyle. Their church is dominated by elders who do not speak English and allow little freedom for young people to determine their own form of worship and youth activities. Myung-Ho and his friends have reacted by refusing to attend church, and the conflict between generations has been painful for all.

Mr. and Mrs. Kim love their son, work hard, and sacrifice much to save for his college education. They want him to succeed in America, be a good Christian, and remain loyal to Korean ways. Myung-Ho respects his parents and their efforts on his behalf, but he has deep-felt needs to be accepted by his Anglo-American peers. Because they have sacrificed much for him, his parents demand that he meet their expectations. He feels they are sacrificing his happiness for outmoded Korean values and mores that, he believes, are out of place in the new country. His parents make obedience to authority and acceptance of Korean customs equivalent to faithfulness to God and the Christian faith. He feels like rejecting Christianity because his church is so legalistic and restrictive.

While this intergenerational conflict is typical of immigrant families, it occurs in other families as well. Parents may sacrifice their children's happiness and emotional well-being on the altar of strict, insensitive demands for conformity to the rules and norms of an earlier day. Can we let God's Spirit help us accept our children as they are and train them so they can make decisions that would please God and enrich their life?

Abraham was following what he thought was God's will, but God was showing him a new and better way. Human sacrifice was outmoded, and God offered an alternative. Could it be that some of our religious and moral practices, which served us well in an earlier day, now need to be reexamined and replaced? God spoke these words to Israel through Isaiah:

> "Do not remember the former things,
>   or consider the things of old.
> I am about to do a new thing;
>   now it springs forth, do you not perceive it?"
>   (Isaiah 43:18-19).

God did a new thing with Abraham and taught him that he could serve God faithfully and at the same time spare and nurture his son. God may be wanting to do a new thing with the Kims and teach them that love for both God and Myung-Ho requires more flexibility and acceptance of new ways. And God may be wanting to do a new thing with us, calling us to be open to fresh possibilities of faithfulness and love of family and church in a new and changing age.

3

The Ten Commandments
Exodus 20:1-17

Then God spoke all these words:
I am the LORD your God, who brought you
out of the land of Egypt, out of the house of
slavery; you shall have no other gods before me.
Exodus 20:1-3

WORDS FOR BIBLE TIMES

Moses has led the people of Israel out of bondage in Egypt.
They have been slaves of Pharaoh but now are nomads,
a straggling band that needs to be formed into a people with a
common identity. The God who delivered them must now
mold them into a nation. They need a sense of boundaries,
direction, and character as a people. They need a covenant
that will bind them to one another and to their God.

Moses meets God on Mount Sinai and receives the Ten
Commandments, which determine who they are to be and how
they are to behave as a people of God. While meant as a
covenant to tie the people of Israel to their God Yahweh, they
are as valid now as then as a guide for conduct and relationships
in human society. The covenant is grounded in the mighty act
of God in bringing the people out of Egypt. Because God has
saved them from a life of oppression, the people are to respond
with gratitude and worship of God (Commandments 1 through
4) and care and responsibility for one another (5 through 10).

The first commandment prohibits polytheism. There is to be
no worship of any god but Yahweh. Since each nation in the
ancient Near East had its own deities, and since people equated

a nation's military success and material prosperity with the power of that nation's gods, the Hebrews would be tempted to switch their loyalty to the gods of the mightiest nation. But Israel was bound by this covenant to follow Yahweh alone.

The second commandment bans idolatry. The Hebrews are not to worship images of any material, animal, or human object set up in place of the one true God. The God of Israel was a Spirit who could not be represented with forms made by human hands. Those who faithfully serve this God will be blessed, while those who worship false gods will be punished.

The third commandment forbids the dishonoring of God's name. The sacred name of God is not to be used in magical incantations, curses, exclamations, or trivial conversation.

The final commandment dealing with obligations to God is the fourth, which requires Israel to honor the seventh day, the day God rested after completing creation. Because the sabbath day has been consecrated by God, God's people must also rest on that day. Sabbath creates a rhythm that renews both body and spirit and gives one a serenity and resurgence of energy to face the demands of the next week.

The next six commandments focus on human relationships, first commanding respect for parents and then prohibiting murder, adultery, stealing, lying, and coveting. To honor God and keep the covenant, people must esteem their parents, respect human life and property, be faithful in marriage, tell the truth, and not crave or seize other people's things.

Jesus reformulates the commandments from negative taboos to positive attitudes: " 'You shall love the Lord your God with all your heart, and with all your soul, and with all your mind. ' . . . And . . . 'You shall love your neighbor as yourself' " (Matthew 22:37-39).

WORDS FOR OUR TIME

The Ten Commandments are so familiar to us that many of us have memorized them and see them as a basic guide for living. Why are we studying them as a troublesome passage?

In the church they are accepted as authoritative; but in society they are disregarded as archaic, developed for a time when life was simple, society was uniform, and people accepted a common standard of behavior. We are so caught up in a climate of individualism and self-fulfillment that we are concerned only with our rights and privileges, not with responsibilities. We are influenced by entertainment figures and public officials who show little regard for the needs and rights of others and even the public good. "If it feels right, go for it." "If you want it, buy it." "Everyone has a price." "Get mine first." These attitudes are our only going guidelines.

In addition to this contempt for the moral standards of the Ten Commandments, many Christians also see them as too legalistic, saying we should be governed by grace, not law. Most decisions are too complex and ambiguous to be determined by a set of rules. Even the Jewish people, finding the Ten Commandments inadequate by themselves, developed volumes of "mishnah," or commentary on the Law, to interpret and apply the Law to a host of diverse situations.

As Christians we are not bound by rules, for we are saved by grace; and our morality is guided by gratitude to God for redemption and by love for neighbor, which is expressed differently in each situation. We make ethical choices, not in terms of law but by judging what will best express love in a given situation. Jesus' positive summary of the Law, "love God and neighbor," is a better guide in our complicated world than a set of ten rules. Ethics by law is like salvation by works; Paul tells us we are "justified by faith apart from works prescribed by the law" (Romans 3:28).

How then do we respond to this double-sided challenge to the validity of the Ten Commandments—from the secular world saying they are an outdated hindrance to self-gratification, and from Christians who believe that freedom in Christ calls for prayerful, loving choices, not blind obedience to the law?

We can affirm three things about the Ten Commandments—God as the ground of morality, the infinite worth of persons, and the importance of a social covenant.

First, morality is based on a relationship with God. The people of Israel honored the commandments because of their covenant relationship with the One who said, "I am the LORD your God, who brought you out of the land of Egypt" (Exodus 20:2). The God who saved them was the God who wanted them to serve him only and to treat persons with respect and consideration, the God who would hold them accountable.

We can disregard a law we think was made by other fallible humans. The ease with which we violate traffic, tax, or civil law when we think we won't be caught is clear evidence of this attitude. But when we know that God is behind the directions, we pay more attention because we want to please and give reverence to the One who loves and leads us.

Second, the Ten Commandments teach regard for persons as made in the image of God. The charge to honor parents and the prohibitions against killing, adultery, stealing, lying, and coveting are all based on the belief that human beings are of infinite worth in God's sight and therefore to be treated with care, dignity, and respect. We are to do to others as we would have them do to us (Matthew 7:12), which is the positive side of the Exodus ban on human mistreatment.

Finally, our behavior is guided by the social covenant. Israel was bound to observe the commandments because they were *a people*, not just a collection of individuals. The Old Testament judges and prophets rebuked Israel because "all the people did what was right in their own eyes" (Judges 21:25), breaking the covenant. We have responsibility for one another because we belong together in covenant.

Our society is coming apart because we are not willing to discipline ourselves—to pay taxes, to curtail profits, to volunteer time, to help our neighbors, to share our resources—for the sake of the common good. So public schools, health care, social welfare, and public safety in the civic arena are all near collapse. Mission support, ecumenical cooperation, denominational loyalty, and social action by the churches are also near collapse. We need a renewed commitment to the public good, recognizing that we have a common responsibility. The people of Israel live on because they are a covenant people who care for one another and put their mutual well-being ahead of individual interests. The Ten Commandments summon us to such a common purpose and destiny.

WORDS FOR MY LIFE

Jerry was nineteen, lived at home, and attended a commuter college. He was brought up a nominal Baptist, sent but not taken to Sunday school, and attended a Catholic high school. There he was strongly influenced by a young Jesuit priest who taught him theology, took a special interest in him, and "was like Jesus to me." But Jerry was turned off by the idea of papal infallibility (the idea that the Pope is incapable of erring) and the authoritarianism in the church, so he was still skeptical when he went to college.

An event in his sophomore year changed all that. An African American family moved into his all-white neighborhood, and a few nights later a cross was burned on their lawn. The neighbors were shocked into action. Representing several different churches, they gathered in one home, determined that such a thing should not happen in their neighborhood, and went to the Black family to offer support and encourage them to stay. They invited them to their homes for meals and took turns patrolling their house at night.

Jerry was so impressed by this demonstration of Christian solidarity and concern that he began visiting the churches in the neighborhood to see what motivated these people to risk their property values and physical safety to make one family feel welcome. He found a church with the right combination of friendly atmosphere, liturgical dignity, Bible emphasis, and warm-hearted faith, and joined it. When I met him, he had made a faith commitment, been baptized, become active in the church, and was teaching a Sunday school class.

The Ten Commandments had taken on a lived vitality for Jerry. He saw his Christian neighbors, motivated by their faith in God, concern for neighbor, and commitment to the common good, band together to take concrete action to offer love, respect, and protection for a neighbor in need.

Whether we view the Ten Commandments as archaic and irrelevant or God-ordained and forever valid, as limiting our freedom or guiding our lives, as equal in authority with or only prelude to Jesus' summary of the Law as "love God and neighbor"—we, like Jerry, can see their fruits in other lives and can be led to a commitment to witness Christ.

So the Ten Commandments, while troublesome to some people, can also be, as the apostle Paul described the Law, "our schoolmaster to bring us unto Christ, that we might be justified by faith" (Galatians 3:24, King James Version) as well as a reliable guide to faithful living.

4

Why Do Innocents Suffer?

Job 1:13-22

Naked I came from my mother's womb, and naked shall I return there; the LORD gave, and the LORD has taken away; blessed be the name of the LORD.

Job 1:21

WORDS FOR BIBLE TIMES

The Book of Job addresses the problem of undeserved suffering. How can a God who is both good and powerful let good people suffer and bad people prosper? It is a powerful drama and is organized like this:

Job 1–2—Prose prologue: Job's misfortune

Job 3—Job's opening speech

Job 4–27—Job's dialogues with friends

Job 28–37—Monologues:

quest for wisdom (28)

Job's defense and oath (29–31)

Elihu's rebukes and proclamations (32–37)

Job 38:1–42:6—Dialogues with God

Job 42:7-17—Epilogue: Job's restoration

The portion considered in this lesson (1:13-22) describes Job's troubles. It is preceded by a portrayal of Job's uprightness, prosperity, and faithfulness in making offerings to God (1:1-5). Then follows a scene in the heavenly court, in which, after God praises Job's virtue, Satan challenges God to take away all his sources of happiness: "Stretch out your hand now, and touch all that he has, and he will curse you to your face" (1:11). God is so sure that Job will be faithful in any trial that he permits this testing.

Here begins a series of calamities in Job's life. His oxen and donkeys are killed; his sheep and servants are burned; his camels are driven off and their drivers murdered. Then his children are all killed by a tornado. Job is so upset by all these disasters that he tears his robe, shaves his head, falls to the ground, and worships God in the words quoted above. But Satan is confounded, for "In all this Job did not sin or charge God with wrongdoing."

Back in the heavenly court God confronts Satan with the news that Job "still persists in his integrity, although you incited me against him, to destroy him for no reason" (2:3). But Satan gains God's permission to afflict Job with sores from head to foot.

Job's wife mocks him: "Do you still persist in your integrity? Curse God, and die" (2:9). But Job remains faithful: "Shall we receive the good at the hand of God, and not receive the bad" (2:10)?

Although Satan has failed to cause Job to renounce God, Job has lost all. So his friends Eliphaz, Bildad, and Zophar try to console him.

The prologue suggests that the innocent suffer because of Satan's malicious interference in God's good plan for the well-being of the faithful. But the rest of the drama offers other explanations of this dilemma that has long troubled humankind. The three friends contend that Job must have sinned, because all suffering is punishment for wrongdoing. So they urge Job to examine his heart and repent. But Job still protests his innocence. Elihu rebukes both the friends for their foolish advice and Job for his pride and then affirms God's goodness and majesty, which overshadow human suffering. Then God points out Job's arrogance before the glory of creation.

Job humbly confesses his humanness:
"I have uttered what I did not understand,
　　things too wonderful for me,
　　　　which I did not know" (42:3).

In the epilogue, Job's friends are humiliated and his fortunes are restored. Virtue is rewarded in the end, Job's story seems to say.

WORDS FOR OUR TIME

A long-awaited baby is born with muscular dystrophy. A beloved spouse is rendered inactive by a stroke. A saintly Christian agonizes with bone cancer. An honest, hard-working merchant loses his business. A devoted spouse is left by husband or wife for another partner. A small nation fighting high poverty and unemployment is hit by a ruinous earthquake. A tiny child is orphaned by a plane crash. A crack baby faces a disadvantaged future. A polio victim on crutches is struck down by a speeding automobile. The list could be endless. *Why, oh why, we cry, do the innocent have to suffer?*

And the other side of the question—why do the wicked prosper?—is equally distressing. How can a God who is both good and all-powerful allow such inequities? Where is justice? It is not Job who disturbs us by raising this issue; it is the unfairness in life itself that is troubling. The Book of Job simply tries to help us resolve the question.

Human beings have wrestled with this issue since time began. Here are some of their explanations:

1. *Many evils are caused by the misuse of human freedom.* The mother of a crack baby, the driver who doesn't see the man on crutches, the plane mechanic who forgets to check a crucial procedure—these sometimes sinful, sometimes mistaken actions of limited, fallible, self-centered, disadvantaged human beings cause much undeserved suffering.

2. *Some suffering is punishment for sin.* Job's friends were partly right. We bring some misfortune on ourselves. Flagrant violation of healthy eating and drinking habits is hazardous. Physical or mental abuse will in time provoke a reaction. Speeding is risky. Smoking causes cancer. We cannot violate God's laws of nature and relationships without facing the consequences sooner or later.

3. *Suffering is good discipline.* Hardship develops character. We become better persons with deeper faith through dealing with loss, pain, handicap, and illness. The Letter to the Hebrews says, "Endure trials for the sake of discipline. God is treating you as children; for what child is there whom a parent does not discipline? . . . We had human parents to discipline us, and we respected them. Should we not be even more

willing to be subject to the Father of spirits and live? . . . He disciplines us for our good. . . . Now, discipline always seems painful rather than pleasant at the time, but later it yields the peaceful fruit of righteousness" (Hebrews 12:7-11).

4. *Suffering is needed as a contrast to pleasure.* Life would be boring and monotonous if people faced no hardship or challenge. A level plain lulls us to sleep, while a hilly road with bumps and turns makes the trip more interesting. We don't really appreciate our good fortune if we have no disappointments or setbacks. The shadows in a painting throw its bright spots and figures into bold relief. God gives us the hard times to make us more grateful for life's blessings.

5. *Suffering is the necessary prelude to new life and hope.* This is the message of the cross. God has brought redemption and abundant life through Christ's death. It takes suffering to engender new life. Spring would not be joyous without the barrenness of winter. Only through the pains of childbirth can an infant be born. The creation of a poem, sonata, invention, or cathedral requires struggle. Nothing worthwhile in life is easy. "Unless a grain of wheat falls into the earth and dies, it remains just a single grain; but if it dies, it bears much fruit" (John 12:24). "If any want to become my followers," said Jesus, "let them deny themselves and take up their cross and follow me. For those who want to save their life will lose it, and those who lose their life for my sake . . . will save it" (Mark 8:34-35). There can be no resurrection without a crucifixion.

Each of the above responses throws some light on the mystery of innocent suffering. None by itself provides the whole answer. Only God sees the whole picture. "We'll understand it better by and by."

WORDS FOR MY LIFE

Ken, Ellen, and their daughter, Naomi, were an ideal family. Ken, 54, was a competent lawyer, well respected in his profession, and a member of the local school board. An active church member, he saw both his work and his community service as expressions of his Christian vocation. Out of a deep sense of calling to lay ministry, Ellen, an ex-school teacher, had gone to seminary, then taken a responsible position in a church agency, and become active in conference church work. Naomi had just graduated from college, gone on a Volunteers in Mission project to Central America, and begun working in a youth service agency.

Early one morning Ken had a severe stroke and was rushed to the hospital where he lay in a coma for two days. Friends and family joined Ellen and Naomi in a prayerful vigil at his bedside. When tests showed that though still breathing Ken was brain dead, Ellen bravely decided to have the life supports removed. Holding back tears, she spoke eloquently of her love for Ken, her grief at his sudden seizure, and her confidence that his stricken body could no longer contain his spirit. In just minutes he was gone.

Now for Ellen and Naomi began the long, lonely adjustment to life without their beloved Ken. It has now been over two years since they lost him, and outwardly they seem to be doing fine. But when a loved one goes, a piece of oneself goes too. The gap in their hearts—and in their church and community—will never be filled.

Why? Why does someone with so much to give, so much of life still to live, such deep faith and solid Christian character, have to die so young? Why does such a close, loving family have to be broken up prematurely? Why do a church and community that so much needed and benefited from Ken's leadership have to be deprived of his contribution?

Job's story does not directly answer the question of innocent suffering. However, it does help Job understand his creaturehood and mortality. He comes to know that God is real and accessible to the people who call upon God and that God is present in their struggle to face and overcome suffering.

5

The Potter and the Clay
Jeremiah 18:1-11

J ust like the clay in the potter's hand, so are you in my hand, O house of Israel.

Jeremiah 18:6

WORDS FOR BIBLE TIMES

The nation of Judah has sinned by worshiping the gods of neighboring nations, by practicing injustice and exploiting the poor, by taking pride in their own merit and not acknowledging God's mercy and providence, and by presuming that because they were chosen they could do what they pleased and God would protect them.

But history has caught up with them. As Israel, their sister nation to the north, had fallen to the Assyrians over a century before, now a new enemy, Nebuchadnezzar of Babylon, has invaded their land, and laid siege to Jerusalem. But King Zedekiah, his counselors, the prophets, and most of the people are not worried. The God who rescued them from slavery in Egypt is on their side and will deliver them again. As the chosen people, they lead a charmed life.

Only Jeremiah is not convinced. Or rather, he *is* convinced—that the Babylonians have been sent by God to call the chosen people to repentance. But he is like a voice crying in the desert. No one will listen, and he is accused of treason for predicting that, as punishment for their sin, Jerusalem will fall, many will die, and the rest will be taken into exile.

God has called Jeremiah to speak an unpopular message that questions prevailing assumptions, conveying it through familiar images and symbolic acts. One such symbol is the potter and the clay. While walking through the potters' street in Jerusalem, Jeremiah sees the parallel between the potter who shapes, crushes, and then reshapes clay into pots, and the God who, having once created Israel as a nation, can undo and remake her to serve the divine purpose. If the people refuse to cooperate and serve God faithfully, God will break them up and later reshape them in a new way.

Jeremiah saw a potter crush down a spoiled pot and rework the clay "into another vessel, as seemed good to him." Just as the potter could do this with clay, so could God "pluck up and break down and destroy" the wayward nation of Judah. "But if that nation . . . turns from its evil, I will change my mind about the disaster that I intended to bring on it." God tells Jeremiah to proclaim to the people of Jerusalem, "Look, I am a potter . . . devising a plan against you. Turn now, all of you from your evil way, and amend your ways and your doings." If Judah will repent and turn to God, they will be spared. But if they persist in their sinful ways, the divine potter will crush the flawed pot and start over to fashion the clay in a way more pleasing to him.

WORDS FOR OUR TIME

Jeremiah's parable seems to suggest that persons and nations are just clay in the potter's hand, putty to be shaped by God with no voice or will of our own. We are not free to make responsible choices but must submit to God's molding and direction. History is predetermined. If we attempt to chart our own course and it does not please God, God will force us back into line, break up the faulty pot and start over. Are our lives and the destinies of nations really controlled in this way? Is our freedom of choice really an illusion? Does God want us to be pliable clay with no real will of our own, spineless and compliant? This is the troublesome aspect of this image of the potter and the clay.

Many women are particularly disturbed by the notion of Christian discipleship as submission and obedience. Women have been conditioned to play this role, and they are tired of it. They cannot accept being relegated to subservient status.

This is dehumanizing and demeaning of the image of God in which all are created. They do not believe that God wants them to deny themselves if that means subjection to male figures, whether human or divine. They—and many men as well—feel called into relationships of mutuality, partnership, and shared ministry. They worship a God of liberation and love, not of lordly domination. They see power as freeing and empowering, not as confining and controlling.

For them Christian discipleship is not selfless submission to a divine autocrat—often represented by an authoritarian, patriarchal church. Rather, they see it as joyous, willing self-giving to a loving Savior, through an accepting, compassionate community, toward the vision of a just, equitable commonwealth in which all persons are treated with dignity and respect. Responsible discipleship is not to be clay in the Potter's hand but to be trusted to make free choices, to be forgiven when these choices turn out wrong, and to be partners with God in the mission of mending creation.

Can the clay be partner with the Potter? Is Christian discipleship a relationship of subject to Ruler or companion with Guide? Some potters speak of a sense in which the clay becomes a live subject in their hands and helps to shape itself. Molding clay is a poetic, intuitive process in which the design is not always preconceived but emerges relationally. Making pots is a spiritual venture in which potter and clay appear to merge together, mutually influence each other, and together form what they are guided into. Each seems to contribute to a common process, yielding a result that neither fully planned or expected. Creation in this instance is not foreordained or premeditated. Potter and clay are each influenced by the other, and both are transformed by the interaction. Generally, though, the potter makes what the market demands, and the clay has not much to say or do about it.

Jeremiah's potter and clay thus become a powerful example for the message he was called to give to Judah. God was demanding absolute obedience with a threat of destruction if the nation did not turn from evil and if the people refused to amend their ways and doings. The clay (the people of God), however, was not an inanimate lump of mud. This was a nation—a living, breathing people who had taken a direction against the will of God for them. God could destroy them anytime. But God is giving them a chance to respond. God wants their cooperation in helping them become a God-loving nation.

WORDS FOR MY LIFE

Laura is an intentional woman in an intentional church. In her early fifties, she feels called to be a junior high teacher and is a very good one. The first high moment in her journey of faith came in confirmation class where she had to memorize the catechism and then be questioned alone before the congregation on a day just for her, which made her feel personally commissioned to follow Christ. From that point on, she took an active role in the life of the church, teaching Sunday school and singing in the choir.

In college Laura intentionally sought a relationship with an active Christian who also had a call to teaching, and they have been committed church members together ever since their marriage. She was delighted when her pastor invited her to teach confirmation class with him, as it brought full circle the experience that had awakened her faith and gave her the opportunity to work with the youth she was especially gifted to reach. Later a pastor persuaded her to leave her teaching career to become educational assistant in their church, a job for which Laura was well suited. But after two years of this, she felt she was betraying her calling to lay ministry in the secular realm; so she returned to junior high teaching.

It might appear that Laura's early formation in home, Sunday school, and confirmation class was a sign of her being passive clay in the Potter's hand. She has been in church as long as she can remember, and her faith and life have been so much influenced by the church that she even goes regularly into the sanctuary to have her time of prayer and devotion. Her character and values have been profoundly shaped by the Spirit of God working through the Christian congregation.

But Laura also is a very self-reliant and deliberate woman. She chose the man she wanted to marry. She chose the career she wanted to pursue. She chose to remain a Christian when a devastating family situation nearly swept her away. She chose to take a "sabbatical" from all church duties when she was feeling burned out. And then she chose to return when she felt ready. She influenced her congregation to take an intentional stance about being a "church for pilgrims" rather than to panic when so many members kept moving away.

While responsive to the formative touch of the Potter, Laura also pushes back and blends her gifts, intelligence, and will with the Spirit's guidance in shaping her life. Her decisions are not reached without doubt and struggle; and sometimes, as with her two-year detour into "full-time church work," she makes a wrong choice. But she remains both open to God's leading and clear about her life goals. So together the Potter and clay mold the pot that is her life journey. The pot is not without blemish, but it holds the water of life that is regularly poured out into the hearts and lives of junior high youth and others touched by Laura's ministry.

God reaches out to touch and mold each of us—and our congregations, communities, and nations. Each must decide how to respond. Will we passively submit, defiantly resist, or actively engage with the Potter in designing and shaping the pot that is our life?

Jeremiah used the image of potter and clay to call rebellious Judah to repent and return to harmony with God's purpose. If we have lost touch with the Potter, such a radical reversal may be necessary for us as well. Or we may need only a more attentive, responsive participation in the molding process. To be "clay in the potter's hand" need not mean being reduced to inert matter subjected to callous manipulation. Rather, it can be felt as a marvelous blending of human and divine wills in a creative, open-ended venture—the forming of a life.

6

True and False Religious Leaders
Ezekiel 34:1-16

I myself will be the shepherd of my sheep, and I will make them lie down, says the Lord GOD. I will seek the lost, and I will bring back the strayed, and I will bind up the injured, and I will strengthen the weak, but the fat and the strong I will destroy. I will feed them with justice.

Ezekiel 34:15-16

WORDS FOR BIBLE TIMES

In the Old Testament the image of shepherd is used to refer to the kings and leaders of the people, those in power and authority. Israel's leaders were called by God to care for their people as a shepherd cares for the sheep. Shepherds are also seen as spiritual overseers (Numbers 27:16-17; Ecclesiastes 12:11; John 21:15-17), appointed by God to guide and nurture the congregation.

Ancient deities were also thought of as shepherds who protect and care for their people (Genesis 48:15; 49:24). Psalm 23 is well-known for referring to God this way, but the shepherd image for God also appears in Psalms 28:9; 74:1; 77:20; 80:1; 95:7; 100:3; in Isaiah 40:11; 49:9-10; Jeremiah 31:10; 50:17-19; and in Micah 4:6-8; 7:14.

In this study the unfaithfulness of Israel's rulers is contrasted with the gentle, loving care of God, who will both tend the sheep and judge the self-serving, negligent shepherds. God orders Ezekiel to speak out against Israel's leaders and to charge them with a list of offenses.

They have fed themselves and not the sheep. They have not upheld the weak, healed the sick, bound up the crippled, or sought the lost. They have ruled by cruel domination, not with compassionate restraint. They have let their people worship false gods at the hilltop shrines and weakened the nation by scattering them abroad (Ezekiel 34:6). They have allowed the people (sheep) to become victims (prey) of invaders and impostors (wild animals) and have been too involved with selfish interests to defend and lead them. Because power has gone to their heads and they have abused their position by exploiting those they were supposed to protect, God will remove them from power and rescue the people from their mistreatment. God himself will become their shepherd, seeking the lost, restoring the strayed, binding up the lame, fortifying the weak, and returning justice to the land.

Human leaders cannot be trusted with unlimited power because power corrupts. Our ultimate loyalty belongs only to God and not to any nation, institution, or political or religious leader. All human agencies, however much they may promise or inspire, are subject to temptation, abuse, and corruption. Only God can provide unfailing love, guidance, and justice.

Ezekiel knew this, warned of the corruption of their leaders, and promised God's salvation from their betrayal. But not until the coming of Jesus was this promise fulfilled in a Good Shepherd who brought abundant life by laying down his life for the sheep and inviting people of all nations to come into one community of faith and peace (see John 10).

WORDS FOR OUR TIME

Is any political or religious leader worthy of trust? So many have been found to have feet of clay (Daniel 2:33). Because of the poor moral judgment of some political and religious leaders, many "true believers" have become disillusioned and lost their faith. Today's passage is troublesome because it reminds us that leaders, however admirable and promising, are disturbingly prone to let us down. Ezekiel warns against this trait of leaders to abuse their trust and of followers to lack vigilance, and about this trait we must be wary.

Ezekiel 34 offers several criteria for distinguishing between true and false shepherd-leaders. Leaders and followers must choose between the following alternatives in determining their relationship:

1. *Will we focus on serving ourselves or serving the people?* "Ah, you shepherds of Israel who have been feeding yourselves! Should not shepherds feed the sheep?" Watch out for pastors and politicians who seek benefits for themselves at the expense of their followers. Signs of this tendency are preoccupation with rewards, concern about being addressed by formal titles, having a reserved parking space, and avoiding the menial aspects of service. Jesus washed the disciples' feet and said, "I am among you as one who serves" (Luke 22:27). Paul reminded the Galatians, "Do not use your freedom as an opportunity for self-indulgence, but through love become slaves to one another" (Galatians 5:13). Who benefits from our leadership?

2. *Will we use power to dominate and control or to strengthen and heal?* "You have not strengthened the weak, you have not healed the sick, you have not bound up the injured, you have not brought back the strayed, you have not sought the lost, but with force and harshness you have ruled them." Strong, visionary leadership is important. But strength is gauged by willing participation in common ventures, not by coerced compliance. Jesus did not thrust nets into the disciples' hands or hang crosses on their backs, but issued gentle, persuasive invitations: "Follow me, and I will make you fish for people" (Matthew 4:19). "If any want to become my followers, let them deny themselves and take up their cross and follow me" (Mark 8:34).

When the disciples of John the Baptist asked, "Are you the one who is to come, or are we to wait for another?" Jesus pointed to the signs of his empowering ministry: "The blind receive their sight, the lame walk, the lepers are cleansed, the deaf hear, the dead are raised, and the poor have good news brought to them" (Matthew 11:3-5). These signs are just the opposite of the marks of the false shepherd-leaders Ezekiel denounced. Are persons uplifted or repressed by our leadership style?

3. *Will our leadership scatter or unite?* "My sheep were scattered over all the face of the earth, with no one to search or seek for them." "I will seek out my sheep. I will rescue them from all the places to which they have been scattered." Some leaders take pride in their skill to "divide and conquer." Keeping people quarreling among themselves leaves the leader free to pursue his/her own objectives. But the church is the *body* of Christ. "For just as the body is one and has many members, and all the members of the body, though many, are *one body,* so it is with Christ" (1 Corinthians 12:12, italics added). Jesus, the Good Shepherd, sought out the "other sheep that do not belong to this fold" and declared, "I must bring them also. . . . So there will be *one flock,* one shepherd" (John 10:16, italics added). Does our leadership antagonize and divide or include and unify?

4. *Will our leadership contribute to just or unjust systems and structures?* "I will bind up the injured, and I will strengthen the weak, but the fat and the strong I will destroy. I will feed them with justice." It is not enough to bind up wounds and comfort the suffering. We must name the *causes* of their misfortune, oppose the exploiters, change oppressive structures, and create fair systems that feed their dignity and well-being. Justice will be meted out according to how well we have "fed them with justice." Is our leadership just—defending the weak, confronting the powerful, and fairly distributing goods and services to all?

These are Ezekiel's guidelines for the kind of sound, constructive leadership that develops persons in the image of God and equips "the saints for the work of ministry, for building up the body of Christ" (Ephesians 4:12).

WORDS FOR MY LIFE

A leader who fit these criteria was Myles Horton, founder of Highlander Folk School, which trained poor, working, and minority persons in the South. In the 1930's and 1940's it organized workers in the labor movement. In the 1950's and 1960's it focused on civil rights and trained African Americans like Rosa Parks to lead the sit-ins, boycotts, and freedom rides. In the 1970's and 1980's, Highlander provided resources to Appalachian people on land rights, pollution, and strip-mining.

Horton describes the purpose of Highlander, now known as the Highlander Research and Education Center, as "to try to contribute toward a genuine democratic society through radical social, economic, political, and cultural change in this country." [1] He says they hoped to interest people in unions and cooperatives as one way to build a democratic society. One of their foundational beliefs is that change in society must come from the bottom up, so they seek to help people struggle to gain their own freedom.

Myles Horton paid a price for his brave, visionary leadership. He said that if those who are struggling for freedom are not facing resistance from the people in power, then they must be working against their own cause. Those who are struggling will always be harassed by those who want to protect the status quo. He had broken ribs, a fractured skull, a broken collarbone, and other injuries. Because it integrated black and white people, Highlander was investigated, raided, and burned. But it continues to this day, developing local leadership.

Horton summed up his ministry this way: "You can challenge people, you can build with people. . . . And if you don't, it seems to me you're minimizing the humanity of people." [2]

Myles Horton was a shepherd-leader who served the poor by strengthening and uniting them to struggle for more just, democratic systems. He respected, loved, and suffered for those he served; and he helped them achieve an abundant life. He meets all of Ezekiel's criteria for good leadership.

How do we assess other leaders—political and religious—in terms of these standards? How do we measure our own leadership, and that of the pastors and officials of our congregations and communities, in their light? What would Ezekiel say today about the leadership of these persons?

---

[1] From *Cloud of Witnesses*, edited by Jim Wallis and Joyce Hollyday (Orbis Books, 1991); page 95.
[2] From *Cloud of Witnesses*; page 103.

7

Will We Always Have the Poor With Us?

Amos 8:4-8

Hear this, you that trample on the needy,
and bring to ruin the poor of the land. . . .
Surely I will never forget any of their deeds.

Amos 8:4, 7

WORDS FOR BIBLE TIMES

Amos was a shepherd and pruner of sycamore trees. While he was tending his flock, God called him to prophesy (Amos 7:14-15). The call probably came through the visions in 7:1–8:3. Amos lived during the reign of Jeroboam II, around 750 B.C., a time of affluence and luxury. He went north from Tekoa in Judah to Bethel in Israel to prophesy. There he confronted the high priest Amaziah, who banished him for making trouble. The reigns of Uzziah and Jeroboam II had brought peace and prosperity but also much evil, injustice, and poverty. Some people lived extravagantly, with fine homes, rich food, elegant banquets, and much leisure. This lifestyle brought with it corruption, repression, bribery, and other forms of vice and inequity. The side effect of this affluent system was a growing sector of landless poor, slaves, and day laborers whose poverty subsidized the wealthy elite. Although many well-to-do people were devout, joining in religious ceremonies, paying tithes and offerings, and performing ritual sacrifices, corruption had penetrated the religious system and some rites were licentious and idolatrous. Indeed, Amos had much to denounce.

His message was this: The day of the Lord is coming. It will not bring the blessing you expect but terrible judgment— defeat and conquest by the Assyrians, destruction and exile. Your only hope is to repent, return to God and faithful living, and restore justice to your society. If these conditions are met, God may show mercy on a remnant.

In this study (Amos 8:4-8), Amos vents God's anger against the oppression of the poor and the greed of the merchants. He condemns those who flagrantly disregard the rights and welfare of the needy, take advantage of the peasants, cannot wait for the religious festivals ("the new moon") to end so they can resume making money, practice business fraud, and buy the poor as slaves or indentured servants. God will not allow you to get away with this, says Amos. God's judgment and recompense will cause the land to quake and all to weep.

Amos has earlier proclaimed the positive side of this judgment in 5:21-24, which begins with God's disapproval of hypocritical worship and ends with the exclamation,

"Let justice roll down like waters,
    and righteousness like an ever-flowing stream."

Injustice, exploitation, and poverty have no place in God's community and cannot be covered up by the veneer of popular religion. God wants us to treat one another fairly, help one another in times of hardship, and run a fair economic system in which all can prosper. To fail to do so will bring God's judgment on the nation, for God's ultimate plan for all people is that justice will prevail.

WORDS FOR OUR TIME

The same extreme gap between wealth and poverty exists today as in Amos's time. In the United States, the people living in poverty grew from 12.6 percent in 1970 to 15.2 percent in the 1980's. The bottom 20 percent of the population receive only 5.3 percent of the income, an average of $3,740 per person, while the top 10 percent receive 23.3 percent, an average of $32,875 per person. [1]

---

[1] From *Risking Liberation: Middle Class Powerlessness and Social Heroism*, by Paul G. King, Kent Maynard, and David O. Woodyard (John Knox Press, 1988); pages 42–43.

The poverty line is defined as an income of $13,360 for two parents and two children, $8,790 for a mother and child, and $6,270 for a single elderly person. In the United States, 13.5 percent of the population lives below this line—equal to the combined populations of Indiana, Illinois, Michigan, and Wisconsin. [2]

But statistics do not tell the whole story. The hardships of poverty fall heaviest on single women with children, especially African American and Hispanic women. Poverty also brings health problems, infant mortality, homelessness, race discrimination, unemployment, poor education, inaccessibility to health care, environmental decay, and a sense of fear, exclusion, anger, powerlessness, and loss of hope.

In some other countries the disparity between rich and poor and the problems of poverty are much greater. When poverty is defined as an income of $1 per day, 1.1 billion people are below this level and face a daily struggle to survive. Over forty thousand children die each day from disease and malnutrition—twenty-eight every minute. [3] Thus, 20 percent of the world's people lack the basic necessities of life. Many of them are unemployed, refugees, and victims of war, pollution, land expropriation, contaminated water, and inequitable distribution of food.

Why is this so, and why have poverty and injustice increased so drastically in recent years? Some fault the poor themselves, saying they are lazy, shiftless, and lack ambition. Others cite the population explosion, maintaining that the earth's resources cannot sustain so many people. Some claim we can produce enough food to sustain an expanding population but blame an inefficient, unjust distribution system. Others hold flawed economic systems accountable, accusing communism of subverting the incentive to work and capitalism of concentrating wealth in the hands of the few.

But Amos points to the real root of the problem—human greed. He condemns those who yearn to sell on the sabbath, "practice deceit with false balances," and are "buying the poor for silver." The apostle Paul bolsters this view with his biting

---

[2] From *Do Justice: Linking Christian Faith and Modern Economic Life*, by Rebecca M. Blank (United Church Press, 1992); page 28.

[3] From *Do Justice*; page 36.

comment, "The love of money is a root of all kinds of evil" (1 Timothy 6:10). And Jesus warns us to "be on your guard against all kinds of greed; for one's life does not consist in the abundance of possessions" (Luke 12:15).

Amos reminds us that religious practice without just behavior offends God, and he cautions us that God will judge those who "trample on the needy, / and bring to ruin the poor of the land." How does God view our vast economic inequities? Are we liable for the same judgment as was Israel? How can we justify having so much when others have so little? Can we claim to have a true faith when we allow this misery to continue? What is God calling us to do to correct these injustices and relieve the plight of the poor?

WORDS FOR MY LIFE

Christians have responded in different ways to the challenge of poverty and injustice in our midst. Few responsible Christians take Jesus' saying "you always have the poor with you" (Matthew 26:11) to mean that the problem of poverty is inevitable and can therefore be ignored.

Clint Decker was vice president for personnel in a big insurance company. Concerned about the lack of opportunity for employment and advancement for women and members of minority ethnic groups, he planned with others in his company to change the company's policies. In three years he brought in and promoted so many women and members of minority ethnic groups that the president became nervous, and Clint was called in and fired. Needless to say, this was a blow, but his lay ministry support group sustained him until he found a job as president of a smaller company and started the same hiring practices there. Clint cared enough about marginalized people to put his job on the line to help improve their situation, and he paid the price for it.

Dolores Huerta, a child of migrant parents who is now vice president of the United Farm Workers union, has devoted her life to organized, nonviolent efforts to improve wages and working conditions for migrant Hispanic laborers. Mother of eleven and grandmother of ten, she serves as the union's chief negotiator, lobbyist, spokesperson, and strategist. She has worked in the fields; lived as a worker; and been beaten, hospitalized, exploited, and poisoned by pesticides. Her response to the need of poor farmworkers has been to share their life, join their struggle, to take part in sympathy fasts, organize strikes and boycotts to pressure growers to provide just working conditions, and to try to raise our awareness to stand in solidarity with them. [4]

These two Christians have taken poverty seriously and have done something about it. What can we do?

1. *We can live simply.* We can avoid conspicuous consumption, conserve the resources of both ourselves and the environment, and identify with the poor in our lifestyle.

2. *We can give.* We can be good stewards of our assets in terms of both frugal spending and gifts to causes that work for justice and equality for poor and marginalized people.

3. *We can put quality above quantity in our own lives.* We can cultivate close friendships; serious conversation; inexpensive recreation; cultural pursuits; solitude and silence; and healthy habits such as jogging, swimming, hiking. Poor people do this of necessity; we can learn from them.

4. *We can work for justice.* We can invest our energies through groups that strive for racial justice; human and civil rights; fair employment and housing; and just laws for labor, immigration, health care, and housing. Volunteer efforts might include writing letters to Congress and newspapers; participating in boycotts and demonstrations; and organizing public meetings, campaigns, and fundraisers.

God through Amos calls us to be aware of and repent for our part in the suffering of the poor, to empathize with them and share in their lives, and to strive to change systems and conditions that perpetuate their misery.

---

[4]From *To Construct Peace*, by Michael True (Twenty-Third Publications, 1992); pages 68–73.

8

Walking With God
Micah 6:6-8

H e has told you, O mortal, what is good;
and what does the LORD require of you
but to do justice, and to love kindness,
and to walk humbly with your God?
Micah 6:8

WORDS FOR BIBLE TIMES

Micah prophesied in the time of Isaiah, during the reigns of Jotham, Ahaz, and Hezekiah of Judah (742–686 B.C.). His name means "Who is like Yahweh?"—in itself a prophetic message of the majesty and power of God. While Isaiah spoke as a high government official, Micah's point of view was that of the common people. He lived in Moresheth, a village in the foothills twenty miles from the Philistine city of Gath. He distrusted city life and saw its moral and spiritual decay as the source of the disaster facing his nation.

His book begins with a judgment on the sins of Israel and Judah, which God will send through the mighty (Micah 1).

Their transgressions are the oppression of the poor and the theft of land from small farmers and peasants by the rich and powerful. Corrupt prophets and greedy priests have cooperated in this unjust system by assuring that no harm can come to God's chosen people. The people of Jerusalem have violated God's purposes and must suffer the consequences (2–3). Yet, even though the nation will be destroyed, Micah sees hope of its restoration, at least for a faithful remnant.

Micah predicts a coming age of peace, justice, and security, in which other nations will seek light from Israel because of its faith in God. After defeat and exile, God will again liberate the people. Through the leadership of a messianic king, God's enemies will be overcome and a penitent, purified remnant will serve God with obedience and virtue (4–5). Until then the people of Israel must remember the love with which God has endured their waywardness and directed their path. Basic to their duty is God's command "to do justice, and to love kindness, / and to walk humbly with your God" (6:8).

This is the core of all prophetic teaching. Formal rites alone will not please God. True religion demands a close relationship with God, caring treatment of others, and upright public conduct. As we saw in the Ten Commandments, the whole Law (and now the prophets as well) is summarized by Jesus in the Great Commandment, "You shall love the Lord your God with all your heart, and with all your soul, and with all your mind, and with all your strength . . . [and] your neighbor as yourself" (Mark 12:30-31).

The demands of heartfelt religion are high, for both moral conduct and purity of worship; and mere humans cannot live up to them in their own strength. But it is Micah's vision that God will provide a way for all people to live together in the kind of community that fulfills the divine purpose and acknowledges God's compassion and power (Micah 6–7). God pardons iniquity, shows compassion, and is faithful to the descendants of Abraham and Jacob (7:18-20).

WORDS FOR OUR TIME

The difficulty with today's passage is not that it is hard to understand. It is very clear: God expects us to live exemplary lives. Nor is the problem that we disagree with Micah's message. Integrity is a central biblical theme: Authentic faith demands both obedience and trust in God and honest dealings with others—love for God and neighbor. The trouble with this passage is that it sets the standards too high for us. Who of us can say that we do justice, love kindness, and walk humbly with our God? What changes would take place in our lives if we really took this instruction seriously?

1. *To do justice would mean that we would*

- see that all get a fair share of the earth's resources;
- treat persons of all races, nations, and classes as we would like to be treated;
- see to it that all people have a roof over their heads, three meals a day, and adequate, affordable medical care;
- be willing to pay higher taxes to make health care, education, housing, and nutrition available to all;
- provide jobs for all people so they could earn their living, support their families, and live with dignity;
- in personal relationships, treat all persons with generosity, fairness, and respect, as children of God;
- use peaceful, respectful, trusting means of settling disputes, and not resort to violence or coercion;
- keep our promises, act honorably and faithfully, and not try to deceive, outwit, or take advantage of others;
- be fair and evenhanded in making decisions and allocating resources; not show partiality, offer favors, or allow ourselves to be improperly influenced;
- "Love your enemies and pray for those who persecute you, so that you may be children of your Father in heaven; for he makes his sun rise on the evil and on the good, and sends rain on the righteous and on the unrighteous" (Matthew 5:44-45).

2. *To love kindness would mean that we would*

- show compassion to the needy—the hungry, homeless, jobless, stateless—by sharing our resources with them;
- forgive others when wronged by them, without getting even or demanding our due;
- go out of our way to help another, even when this is inconvenient, costly, or stressful;
- welcome people into our churches, homes, hearts, and lives, regardless of how we might think they "fit";
- take other people's pain onto ourselves, whether this be physical, emotional, or spiritual;
- accept other people as they are, warts and all, without demanding that they live up to our expectations;
- spend ourselves—our energy, money, and time—to help make others secure, comfortable, and whole;
- "Bear one another's burdens, and in this way you will fulfill the law of Christ" (Galatians 6:2).

3. *To walk humbly with God would mean that we would*
- pray regularly in order to stay close to God;
- allow God's loving Spirit to fill our hearts, direct our lives, and shape our actions and reactions;
- be faithful and dependable in worship attendance and service in and through the church;
- be courageous and steadfast in standing and speaking for God's purpose and against God's enemies;
- be a source of support to others weaker in the faith;
- offer wisdom and guidance to those who seek and those who falter on the way;
- freely acknowledge our own shortcomings and not pretend to be something greater than or different from what we are;
- accept menial assignments and do them willingly and cheerfully, as unto the Lord;
- trust God to stand with us in life's boundary experiences—illness, grief, pain, and death—and face into them in faith, knowing that God is by our side;
- believe, even when outer circumstances do not support our belief;
- be confident that "all things work together for good for those who love God, who are called according to his purpose" (Romans 8:28).

All three lists could be extended; but already we are overwhelmed with what God expects, and we know we cannot measure up. Aware of our shortcomings, we can either despair or turn to God for mercy and strength. The same God who asks much also offers much: "My grace is sufficient for you, for power is made perfect in weakness" (2 Corinthians 12:9). In our own strength we cannot do justice, love kindness, and walk humbly with God. But "if we confess our sins, he who is faithful and just will forgive us our sins and cleanse us from all unrighteousness" (1 John 1:9). Then we "can do all things" through Christ, who strengthens us (Philippians 4:13).

WORDS FOR MY LIFE

One vibrant example of a life in response to Micah's challenge is Dorothy Day, the founder of the Catholic Worker movement. We see in her and this movement a life and a community dedicated to justice and kindness and based on the poverty, simplicity, and vulnerability of Jesus. Through her influence lives were transformed, religious institutions revived, social injustices challenged, and the poor blessed.

She was converted from a life in which she was a radical Marxist, a common-law wife, and an unwed mother, through a period of "long loneliness." She found a deep faith in God that led her to see the world as beautiful and the sacraments as meaningful. Her social concern was grounded in biblical imperatives of justice, goodwill, nonviolence, and peace. An ardent pacifist, she participated in antiwar marches, rallies for racial equality, and prayers for peace.

She formed Christian Worker houses in most major cities and many rural farm cooperatives, where small communities lived in voluntary poverty, shared things in common, offered hospitality to the homeless, practiced organic farming, and planned and agitated for social change. Dorothy and many others in the movement suffered ostracism, vilification, beatings, arrest, and imprisonment for their radical obedience to God's call to a life of kindness and justice.

The life of Dorothy Day was devoted to doing justice, loving kindness, and walking humbly with God. It was rooted in God's grace and presence, which enabled her to live in a strength greater than her own.

We may not be able to live as she did. But God will help us find our own way to do justice, love kindness, and walk humbly with God. The Bible holds up the challenge. The above guidelines help point the way. Our community of faith provides support. The Spirit of God gives power and inspiration. But we all have to make our own choices, chart our course, and persevere on the way.

9

The Beatitudes
Matthew 5:1-12

W hen Jesus saw the crowds, he went up the mountain; and after he sat down, his disciples came to him. Then he began to speak, and taught them.

Matthew 5:1-2

WORDS FOR BIBLE TIMES

M any Christians have looked on these teachings of Jesus as a set of impossible and troublesome standards, and with good reason. They seem to place Christian discipleship well beyond our reach. When we consider them in their biblical context, however, we find that they are not nearly so impossible as they seem.

First of all, the passage makes clear at the outset that Jesus is not addressing a large crowd of people, but his disciples. The crowd may overhear what he has to say (Matthew 7:28-29), but they are not the intended audience. When addressing larger groups of people, Jesus was less demanding. On those occasions he often used parables to make his teachings more accessible.

It is also clear that this was a more intimate setting, because Jesus is identified as a teacher. The word *teach* had a specific connotation in the Jewish rabbinical tradition. It described the instruction received by a small group of students who had made it their priority to learn the mind of their teacher in depth. Since on fourteen occasions in the Gospels Jesus is given the title of rabbi (*rabbouni* in Aramaic), we can be sure that this was the nature of these Beatitudes. So to regard them as rules and regulations would be to misunderstand not only their content but also their purpose.

This same intimacy was found in congregations of the early church, which usually met in people's homes. In an atmosphere of love and mutual commitment, these early Christians quite naturally explored the teachings of Jesus in some depth, seeking for spiritual foundation as well as practical application. After all, they were a household—God's household. In fact, the concept of a household—the building, the people, the resources, and the relationships—are a recurring theme throughout Matthew's Gospel. In such a setting, the dynamic of love implicit in these teachings was by no means impossible. Much of the time, it was a spontaneous reality.

WORDS FOR OUR TIME

To our great disadvantage, this concept of the church as a household is all too rare in our congregational life today. Even in the small membership churches familiar to so many of us, the closeness and familiarity are disappearing.

Of course we make efforts, often vigorous efforts, to promote Christian community among our members. We encourage small groups, we foster Sunday school classes, and we experiment with a succession of programs that are supposed to "bring people closer together." But time and again we find that our efforts are forced rather than spontaneous and short-lived rather than self-generating. Our consumerist culture usually wins the day. In a word, we have become too selfish to share in God's household.

So instead of intimate communities of faith, all too often our churches are formalized. They tend to function much like any other social institution. We may be cordial and supportive of one another, but we rarely plumb the depths of Christ's teachings in our activities or conversation. And even though we follow democratic principles in our church government and organization, many of our congregations lean toward a hierarchical structure. We often find that some people are "in charge" and that everyone else is quite happy to let them assume all the responsibility.

Little wonder that these Beatitudes are difficult to comprehend, still less to follow, in such settings. Without the intimacy of mutual support, mutual oversight, and mutual confession, they can indeed become formalized, idealistic, and even legalistic principles. And when this happens, people often react against most of what Jesus had to say, to the point of avoiding his teachings altogether. "Of course the meek are blessed," we reason, "as are the peacemakers and those who are persecuted for the sake of righteousness. But if that's what I have to do to be a Christian disciple, forget it! I'll just do the best I can, and Jesus will understand."

There must be a better way than this, and there is. The teachings of Jesus are not rules and regulations. They are instructions from a teacher who wants to share with us the love of a parental God who is deeply concerned about our welfare and wants us to live on planet earth in ways that will bring us maximum blessing and joy. To follow the teachings of Jesus in joyful obedience is to know the God who was in Christ, a God who is loving and parental. Put differently, the teachings of Jesus reach into our hearts as well as our minds. They shape not only our words and deeds but our thoughts and motives.

Does this mean, then, that rules and regulations do not count? Does it mean that if large, institutional churches are not conducive to a real understanding of the teachings of Jesus, we should give up on our congregations and form house churches instead?

Not at all. Jesus was not denying the validity of the Law. He was rather teaching his disciples a deeper law—the law of love, God's love. Compared with this law of love, all other laws, rules, and regulations are mere courtesies of human behavior. And while courtesy is commendable, disciples of Jesus must go further and show a better way.

Neither was Jesus denying the validity of religious institutions; he worshiped in synagogues and at the Temple in Jerusalem. Besides, by no means all of his teachings were directed at his disciples. He also had words of grace, power, and healing for other people. They too came to him. He fed them, healed them, and taught them; and his heart went out to them.

People continue to come to our places of worship, Sunday by Sunday and at many other times during the week. They are coming for the same reason—to be fed and healed and taught by Jesus Christ. Our institutional churches must be open and available for these people. We must welcome everyone who will come, and we must be missional outposts of justice and love for those who will not. When they do come, it is our task as Christ's disciples to make sure they are fed and healed and taught and loved, just as the disciples helped Jesus distribute the bread and fish to the five thousand (Matthew 14:19-21). We must introduce them to the teachings of Jesus and to Jesus himself.

WORDS FOR MY LIFE

At this point you may be asking, "If Jesus had two kinds of teaching, one for his disciples (more demanding), and one for other people (less demanding), which kind applies to me? Just as important, where do I fit in at my church? Surely every church member should be a disciple. Does that mean that if I am not ready or able to follow these Beatitudes, I am not a Christian?"

Questions such as these get to the real meaning of our discipleship. Yes, we have a personal relationship with Jesus Christ; but there is much more to discipleship than that. When we become disciples of Jesus Christ, we accept his agenda, an agenda that impels us to reach out to people, especially the poor, the captives, the blind, and the oppressed (Luke 4:18-19). This is why Jesus impressed upon Peter to feed his sheep and lambs (John 21:15-17). Furthermore, the scope of their task was worldwide. They were to make disciples of all nations, teaching them to obey everything he had commanded (Matthew 28:19-20). As the latest disciples of Jesus Christ, we have the same task. As Jesus himself said, merely calling him "Lord, Lord" is not enough (Matthew 7:21).

What the first disciples could not have known, however, was just how long this worldwide teaching would take. Two thousand years have passed, and still the nations of the world are far from obedient to the teachings of Jesus Christ. Indeed, many of the world's Christians are far from being obedient disciples. Jesus knew that this would happen. He knew people would not respond to his teachings right away, that it would take time. He also knew that even when people did respond to his teachings, they would not understand them all at once. That too would take time, and much, much grace.

But Jesus also knew that some disciples would grow in grace to the point where they could be trusted to help with this task of global transformation—women and men who would help feed the hungry, bind up the brokenhearted, and comfort all who mourn (Isaiah 61:1-2; Luke 4:18-19). Persons such as these would be ready to be his *disciplined* followers, plumbing the depths of his teachings and seeking to live them out in the world.

To persons such as these Jesus directs his most demanding teachings. We are indeed blessed when we find them piercing our hearts.

10

Is the Old Testament Relevant?

Matthew 5:17-48

Do not think that I have come to abolish the law or the prophets; I have come not to abolish but to fulfill. . . .

· ·

Be perfect, therefore, as your heavenly Father is perfect.

Matthew 5:17, 48

WORDS FOR BIBLE TIMES

Jesus becomes quite specific in the teachings in Matthew 5:17-48, and he seems to place them altogether beyond our reach by saying that we must be perfect—just like God! This is troublesome indeed!

Once again, however, we must keep these verses within their biblical perspective. When Jesus refers to the Law, he does not mean a set of rules and regulations. He is referring to the Hebrew Torah, a body of law at once more positive and dynamic. Today we tend to think of law as prohibitive or intrusive, like a speed limit on a highway or a penalty on our income tax—something to be avoided if at all possible.

This was not how the Hebrews viewed the Torah. To them it was good news. It was liberating. The Torah was their means of salvation, a pathway out of sin and into a relationship with God, the God who was their deliverer, the God who had brought their forebears out of slavery in the land of Egypt. To the Hebrews the Torah was more than a set of rules, much more.

Jesus affirmed the Torah and then went further. Not only was Torah the law of a righteous God, but it was also the law of a God who was loving and parental. In fact, Torah could be summed up in a single word—God's law of *love*.

This did not mean reducing the law to an emotion. Jesus knew that human self-deception is highly inventive, which is why he stressed that not one letter, not even part of a letter, would be replaced by what he had to say. The letter of the law, however, was not enough. To understand the Torah, one had to seek the will of God that lay behind the Law and the Spirit of God that shaped the Law. Viewed as negative restrictions, the Torah could easily become prohibitive and intrusive. Viewed as an expression of the love of God, it became positive and dynamic.

As Christians we should never forget that the founder of our faith honored his Jewish forebears. Jesus was a teacher in the Jewish rabbinical tradition and a prophet in the tradition of Isaiah (Luke 4:16-21). He not only honored Hebrew tradition; he was excited by it as was any good rabbi. His words tingle with the energy and purpose he found in God's law of saving grace.

And when we place his teachings in the context of the early Christian community in which Matthew's Gospel was written, they are clearly an invitation to share in a family relationship, in a household of justice for all people and of peace between all people. They are the house rules of a God who, then and now, wants us to share in a perfection of love.

WORDS FOR OUR TIME

In the intimacy of the household of God, we can turn to the teachings of Jesus with a sense of expectancy. Our teacher, Rabbi Jesus, is excited about them and wants us to join him in exploring the mind of God.

We sense this early in the passage when Jesus tells his disciples that their righteousness is to exceed that of the scribes and Pharisees. What does he mean by this?

First, we should note that the Hebrew word for righteousness signifies God's kindness and goodness toward the human race. Human righteousness must be an extension of this divine initiative, expressed in kindness and goodness toward our neighbor.

We should also note that the Greek word translated righteousness in this passage can also be translated as justice, a word that Matthew uses more times than all the other Gospels combined. Rather than being a clinical concept of morality, God's righteousness impels us into the world on behalf of those who suffer from the world's injustice—the "sinned-against" who usually remain anonymous because we find their presence discomfiting.

So the intent of the teaching in this passage is clear. Those of us who are disciples of Jesus Christ must do more than merely imitate the scribes and Pharisees. We must do what *God* would have us do—love one another as sisters and brothers in the household of God, and extend God's justice (God's righteousness) to the poor and disadvantaged of the world.

However, this intent does raise a question. Why should Jesus instruct those of us in the household of God to love one another when God's righteousness directs us toward the needy of the world? Is this not telling us to be selfish, perhaps even self-indulgent?

This question has two answers. The first is that family squabbles in the household of God will always distract from our task as Christian disciples and consume much of our energy. Think how often a church committee will decide in two minutes that the poor need to be helped and then spend two hours trying to figure out how not to get cheated in the process. Think how tiring it is to cope with minor misunderstandings in the church when we could be reaching out to those in need beyond it. Jesus is saying that if we would only agree to love one another, we could do so much more for his little ones in the world—and have a much better time being Christian.

The second answer is that, if those of us in the household of God do not live by the house rules, then we deprive ourselves of the grace we need for our discipleship in the world. Indeed, if we persist in breaking the house rules, God cannot use us at all. We become salt without flavor and light that is hidden (Matthew 5:13-16). When we do follow the house rules, however, we begin to see why Jesus was so enthusiastic about them. They make good sense; and when they are practiced according to God's law of love, they have the power to transform the world.

In short, belonging to the household of God brings privilege and responsibility. The privilege is the intimacy and security of family life. The responsibility is that we must leave no room at all for attitudes that disrupt the dynamic of love and distract us from the work Christ has called us to do in the world.

God's house rules reach into the heart and require absolute integrity. There can be no deceit in the household of God, no duplicity, no hypocrisy. Rabbi Jesus is quite firm. Don't even *think* you can be in communion with God if anything is unresolved between you and your sister or brother. Get it resolved, and quickly, for there is work to be done in the world.

How far does God's household extend? Jesus had an answer for that question as well. "A man was going down from Jerusalem to Jericho, and fell into the hands of robbers" (the parable of the good Samaritan, Luke 10:30-37).

WORDS FOR MY LIFE

The more we reflect on these teachings, the more they search our hearts, and the more we realize that we must do our best to live them out in our lives. Because they are teachings for the heart, we know that Jesus accepts our best efforts despite our shortcomings. Because they are also guidelines for daily living, we know that goodwill alone is not enough. We must also put these teachings into practice.

Jesus sees through our excuses and especially that old complaint that we are not good enough to be his disciples. Of course we are not. The point is, Jesus wants us to try anyway. And when we do try, we are given all the strength we need. That is what grace is all about.

Unfortunately, this effort is not always where our church life seems to be focused. We spend our time and energy on committees and programs. Even when we do try to live out the teachings of Jesus, we rarely seem to find the intimate spiritual communion that could give us the grace to love our enemies, pray for those who persecute us, or tremble in fear of calling our brother or sister a fool. It seems as if we deliberately make ourselves busy with congregational life and work to avoid the deeper truths of Jesus.

While every congregation needs to have programs and activities, we know that those of us who are no longer infants in Christ, those of us who are ready to be *disciplined* followers of Jesus Christ, must also have nurture and instruction. When we are called by Jesus to this kind of discipleship, we must plumb the depths of his teachings. And for this to happen, we must seek the company of like-minded Christian friends and colleagues. Together with them we can seek to understand the teachings of Rabbi Jesus in a household setting. Whether we create that setting in someone's home or in the buildings we have come to regard as our church home, we must find the time and space to sit at the feet of Jesus.

11

The Radical Demands of Jesus
Matthew 10:34-39

Do not think that I have come to bring peace to the earth; I have not come to bring peace, but a sword. . . . Those who find their life will lose it, and those who lose their life for my sake will find it.

Matthew 10:34, 39

WORDS FOR BIBLE TIMES

This seems to be a harsh and somewhat contradictory teaching from Rabbi Jesus. He is telling his disciples that they can expect to be rejected by those closest to them, even in their own households, and they are not to be surprised when this happens. His teachings are revolutionary and therefore disturbing and subversive. They will certainly not leave people unmoved.

Where is God's law of love in this teaching? Indeed, it is enough to put one off discipleship altogether.

When we ponder these words, however, we realize that Jesus has not forgotten God's law of love. We have already seen that his teachings were radical. They went to the root of the Torah in affirming an unconditional dependence on God's grace. As with anything radical, these teachings were bound to be disturbing; so Jesus was merely stating the obvious: Christian disciples should expect trouble from the world.

Ironically, early Christian communities experienced this trouble most directly in the area of family life. If one member of a family became a Christian and the others did not, clearly there would be tensions. But even when whole families joined the church, traditional lines of authority, and especially patriarchal authority, came into question. In God's household the only true authority lay with Jesus, whose teachings made all family members equal in the sight of God.

Given the pattern of Jewish family life, to say nothing of Greek and Roman customs, trying to follow the teachings of Jesus would indeed seem to foster disrespect for parental authority, and thereby parental resentment toward disrespectful children. It was important to Matthew for his house church to know that such conflicts were to be expected.

This passage has an even more serious note. Not only will his followers face family tensions, Jesus warns, but those who are worthy of him must also be ready for persecution by the world. They must even be ready for torture and death. This is the first mention of the cross in Matthew, and at that time the cross meant only one thing—a public, painful, and humiliating death. The warning of Jesus is serious. And as the disciples later experienced, it was altogether warranted.

This is the hardest teaching of all, and there is no way to sanitize or sugarcoat it. The life that Jesus offers us is eternal. Since the only way to this life is death, sooner or later, clinging to earthly life at the expense of obedience to God is an act of self-destruction. Why risk the fullness of eternal life for something that is so short-lived? Once again, Jesus is stating the obvious.

WORDS FOR OUR TIME

The teachings of Jesus always have two effects on those of us with ears to hear. The first is to show us the will of God for our lives, a way of love and justice and peace. The second is to reveal the extent of our waywardness by exposing our false gods, our idols. This second effect is the reason for so much disturbance in the lives of Christian disciples. Once we make our commitment to Christ, we are only beginning our pilgrimage of repentance, forgiveness, and grace.

God's judgment on human sin is not that culprits must be found, but that a cure is needed. It is not our fault that we are sinners, but it becomes our fault when we try to deny that we are. It is our self-justification that makes God's cure and course-correction so difficult. Like all children who are lost, we don't want to admit it. We want to wander farther afield, pursuing the attractions that enticed us to leave home in the first place. To be interrupted by a call to turn back is irritating enough. But to be told that the attractions are idolatrous is infuriating. We like these idols. Their rewards seem to be gratifying compared with God's parental concern, which comes across as interference and domination.

Ironically, one of the most powerful idols throughout Christian history has been the human family. The irony lies, of course, in the teachings of Jesus about God's parental qualities and in the household economy of the early church. But Jesus is not asking us to reject our parents or our children to be his disciples. He is rather pointing out that if we love them *more* than we love him, we are not worthy of that status.

For the most part, we find ourselves able to do both. We can love our mother and father, our son and daughter, and at the same time be faithful disciples of Jesus. But we must be ready, warns Jesus, to place our family on hold should he need us for service that our parents or children do not understand, and which costs us their sympathy and support. That's the rub.

If we should have to make this sacrifice, however, there are rich rewards. Once we belong to the extended family of God's household, our relatives multiply many times. Our parents become all those elderly people who want to live their remaining years in dignity but whose collective wisdom is so disdained by our materialistic culture. Our daughters and sons become all those abandoned, abused, and starving children who continue to die across the world at the rate of forty thousand per day. As we join Jesus in this extended family, our relatives may understand or they may not. One thing is clear: Disciples of Jesus of Nazareth ultimately have no choice in the matter. They must "feed my sheep" (John 21:17).

WORDS FOR MY LIFE

These verses hit us like a sledge hammer. And when we have recovered from the blow, we wonder where the joy of our discipleship has gone.

The temptation, of course, is to spiritualize what Jesus has to say and to regard the minor inconveniences of our discipleship as "crosses" to be borne with patience. But the cross that Jesus carried was too real and the martyrs of the church are too numerous for us to take these words at anything less than their face value. The fact is that those who are closest to us—our parents, our children, our best friends—are most often the ones who fail most completely to understand the path of our discipleship. And throughout the world today more Christian martyrs are dying violent deaths for the sake of Jesus and his teachings than at any time in the history of the church.

What if Jesus asks such things of me? The question is enough to put me in a cold sweat. Will I have the courage to stand firm? Will I be able to turn away from my family and leave them to fend for themselves? How will I react if I am required to confront this idol and reject it in the name of Jesus Christ? Most sobering of all, will I be called on to die a violent death for Jesus Christ? Would I have strength to endure such suffering?

As with so much of our discipleship, these questions put the cart before the horse. Two things emerge with some force from the biographies of martyrs in the Jewish and Christian traditions: They found themselves in that position when they least expected it, but once there they were sustained by overwhelming power and grace. The stories of these martyrs tell us that the most important principle of Christian discipleship is not to ask what *might* be required of us but rather to do what *is* required to serve Jesus Christ *here and now* to the best of our ability. As we practice obedience in our routine life and work, we become seasoned in our discipleship. The more faithful we are in the small tasks, the more we are trusted with the larger assignments.

Those who are not worthy of Jesus Christ are not the ones who fail him in times of crisis but the ones who fail to obey him in the minor inconveniences. Persons such as these need not worry about persecution or violent death. Jesus cannot trust them to do *anything.*

Those of us who are faithful need not worry either. As we have learned to be obedient, step by step, we know that we can trust in the grace of Christ to face *everything.*

12

Forgiveness
Matthew 18:21-35

Then Peter came and said to him, "Lord, if
another member of the church sins against me,
how often should I forgive? As many as seven
times?" Jesus said to him, "Not seven times,
but, I tell you, seventy-seven times."

Matthew 18:21-22

WORDS FOR BIBLE TIMES

The parable in Matthew 18:23-35 seems to present a limited view of forgiveness. The Greek word used here is
aphiemi, or "send away," and it is the one used most often in
the Gospels. But the sense of *remit* that we find in this story
lacks the richness of meaning that the word *forgive* has come
to have in Christian teaching and practice.

For one thing, the setting of the parable is quite formal.
This is the remission of a debt owed by a slave to his king. In
the parable the king takes pity on the slave and forgives the
debt, but that is all that happens. There is no reconciliation,
no restoration of family relationships as in the parable of the
prodigal son (Luke 15:20-24).

For another thing, the remission is just as quickly revoked
when the king hears about the forgiven slave's subsequent
behavior.

If we find this story inconsistent with our view of a God
who is loving and parental, it is because we jump too
quickly to conclusions, as we do with so many biblical

words. We assume that God's forgiveness is so readily available that, as soon as we see the error of our ways (or more likely feel sorry for ourselves), we can expect the prompt restoration of our relationship with God, with all the attendant blessings and benefits. But this way of thinking puts matters too much into our own hands. It presumes that we can control the situation and generate God's forgiveness whenever we are ready.

This is not the kind of forgiveness that Jesus was talking about. The parables of Jesus are essentially "one point" stories, and the central point of this parable was to make clear that the prerogative of forgiveness remained with the king at all times. So it is with God. Whenever we repent and turn from our sinful ways, we must never take God's forgiveness for granted. It is true that God is always ready to forgive. We know that God will forgive, because God has covenanted to do so whenever we repent of our sins. But our repentance cannot be mere token regret.

Still less can we assume that forgiveness will automatically bring us all the benefits of God's household. These benefits are another gracious blessing from God and are showered on us with the extravagance of God's parental love. To be forgiven does not mean that we deserve such blessings. It simply means that our sin has been cancelled and that we are now *ready* to receive the blessings. Both these acts—the forgiveness of our sins and the blessings of being reconciled to God's household—are God's prerogative and God's alone.

Why, then, does Jesus make such an issue in this parable and others of our need to forgive those who wrong us? If forgiveness is entirely in God's hands, with our repentance as the only precondition, what do other people have to do with it?

The reason is simple. Repentant persons are bound to look on the sin of others with a marked degree of charity. If we have not forgiven our debtors, we have not searched our own hearts. This is why the part of the Lord's Prayer that mentions forgiving is not a stipulation but an observation (Matthew 6:12). The offense is not only our lack of forgiveness of others. It is the singular bad manners, to say nothing of the impossibility, of trying to negotiate God's forgiveness. No wonder the king was angry with the unforgiving slave. The king had been duped. He had actually believed this man was sincerely repentant.

WORDS FOR OUR TIME

It is difficult to comprehend these teachings of Jesus in our culture today. Compared with the depth of the scriptural meanings we have just explored, our use of the word *forgiveness* is often quite shallow. We live life at such a pace that a whole range of offenses, from unkind words to abusive behavior, are quickly forgotten if renewed cordiality can work to our advantage. Our culture of soap operas and talk shows is a culture in which repentance and forgiveness are merely the price tag for instant and therefore fleeting relationships.

If we are honest, we must admit that the same shallowness has come to permeate a great deal of our church life as well. In the household of God, where relationships ought to be the essence of our life together, we prefer to ignore one another's offenses. After all, it is much less trouble to pretend that nothing has happened or that there was merely a misunderstanding. Perhaps we did not hear one another correctly.

We heard all right. We just don't want to face up to the issue, either as the offender or as the one offended. The problem is that we extend this shallowness to our relationship with God. "I don't mind what happened (meaning, I find it convenient to ignore what happened), so why should God mind?"

Remembering that Jesus was a teacher in the Jewish rabbinical tradition, we must consider another aspect of this passage of Scripture. Peter's question also drew on the Hebrew tradition of communal repentance and forgiveness. The Day of Atonement, on the tenth day of the seventh month, was for the cleansing of all the people's sins; and Peter may well have had in mind the sevenfold sprinkling of blood that was part of this ritual. The prophets and priests did not just call individual persons to repentance. They also called the people of Israel as a nation to turn back to God.

In 1989 a delegation of United Methodists visited the nation of Chile. At that time the country was preparing for its first elections since General Pinochet had come to power in the military coup of 1973. The North Americans were told of the struggle the Chilean Methodists were having over the oppressions of the past fifteen years. Now that political freedom seemed to be close for them, how would they forgive those members of the military government and police who had been responsible for so many abuses?

The questions were poignant, because church members knew many of these men personally and some were even related. "One thing is clear," they said. "We shall of course forgive them. But for us to forgive, there must be an acknowledgment of what was done. We can forgive; but we cannot, and must not, forget."

The social, racial, and economic tensions in the United States in recent decades may not have stemmed from a military dictatorship, but they continue to divide the nation. As Christian disciples, as messengers of the coming reign of God, we must understand that personal sin is only part of the problem. Social sin, economic sin, and systemic sin are likewise an offense to God. We must repent of the sin that is ours by default no less than by design. We must repent of the sin that is ours because of where we live, what we eat, and where we work. Most difficult of all in this day and age is the need to repent for the sins of our forebears. In the United States the most obvious sin in this category is slavery. Indeed, it is still with us. We call it racism.

WORDS FOR MY LIFE

As theologian Stanley Hauerwas has argued in recent years, Christian discipleship is a craft; and forgiveness is one of the most important parts of the craft of Christian discipleship. As with all crafts, it has to be learned. Most especially it has to be learned in the household of God, which is the setting for Peter's question (Matthew 18:21).

Learning forgiveness is not a matter of "getting close" to everyone. On the contrary, we often need solitude in a household, as those of us who grew up with multiple siblings can readily attest. But God's house rules do require us not to allow barriers to remain between ourselves and anyone else. If we are responsible for the barrier, we must repent and ask forgiveness of the one we offended. If our brother or sister in the church is responsible, we must confront the issue, be ready to forgive that person, and do the best we can to be reconciled (18:15-20).

We must understand that God has no favorites. God loves everyone in this household with equal intensity. By definition, therefore, if barriers exist between ourselves and a sister or a brother, they exist between ourselves and God.

All human beings, indeed, all things that live, are loved by God with equal intensity. The whole of planet earth is God's extended family. According to Rabbi Jesus, not only must no barriers exist between human beings but also no barriers between human beings and anything on the earth that gives us life.

When we consider the graciousness of our neighborly animals and plants and the bountiful generosity of the earth, it is clear that we humans have a great deal of repenting to do.

13

Walking in Our Neighbor's Shoes

Matthew 20:1-16

"**T**ake what belongs to you and go; I choose to give to this last the same as I give to you. Am I not allowed to do what I choose with what belongs to me? Or are you envious because I am generous?" So the last will be first, and the first will be last.

Matthew 20:14-16

WORDS FOR BIBLE TIMES

The parable in Matthew 20:1-16 spoke powerfully to the disciples of Jesus and also to the early Christians, many of whom were Jews. The identification of the people of Israel with the laborers who worked all day was quite apparent. For hundreds of years the people of Israel had labored for God, the owner of the vineyard. Not only had they been faithful to the Torah, but they had suffered considerably in doing so. Moreover, when they had erred or disobeyed, they had been rigorously disciplined by God. To say that they had borne the heat of the day was no exaggeration.

So the parable carried a hard lesson for the Jews: They were not the only ones to be favored by God. The Gentiles would also be welcomed as laborers in God's vineyard. And all would be rewarded as God saw fit, even if it seemed unfair to those who had been faithful to God for so long and at such cost.

The early Christians in Matthew's church would likewise have found this a hard lesson. Indeed, it is still a troublesome matter for Christians today. It means that we are not entitled to make any judgment whatsoever about the status, the work, or the reward of anyone else. Be they Jew or Gentile, Christian or pagan, believer or nonbeliever, God and God alone will judge our fellow human beings. And God will judge us.

It was difficult for the Jews to accept Gentiles in the household of God because of the particular covenant relationship between God and the people of Israel. Before they had been exiled in Babylon in the sixth century B.C., they saw their covenant relationship as a divine commission to tell the nations of the world about the one true God (Isaiah 42:5-7). But in the years after the Exile, they came to see the covenant as an exclusive relationship with God. Instead of being chosen by God *for* the nations of the world, they increasingly saw themselves as a people chosen *from* the other nations.

To some extent, this was an understandable reaction to their conquest, exile, and persecution. But this identity was contrary to the spirit of their covenant with God, and Jesus directly challenged it in this parable. Yes, the Jews were God's chosen people; but they were chosen for a purpose and not at the expense of other peoples. And the early Christians had to understand that Jesus had come, not for the selective salvation of a few, but for the salvation of the whole world.

We often draw the same false distinctions today in the church—not between Jew and Gentile, but between those who come to our churches and those who don't. We even try to distinguish between those who are saved and those who are not saved, as if we knew God's mind or as if we were entitled to make God's decisions. Labels such as "churched" or "unchurched," "saved" or "unsaved," must be excised from our Christian vocabulary. They betray the mindset of dissatisfied laborers.

WORDS FOR OUR TIME

During the past twenty-five years in Latin America, groups of Christians have been studying the Bible in a new way. Instead of coming together just for study, they have formed

what are known as *comunidades eclesiais de base*, or base eccle-
sial communities, in which they center their whole life
around the Bible. The word *base* does not mean "basic." It
means that these communities are at the base of human society—at the grassroots. They comprise the common people. In
the view of theologian Leonardo Boff, they are nothing less
than the rebirth of the church in a new form—an *ecclesio-gen-
esis*. The energy and the insights they bring to their reading of
the Bible have become legendary.

Take the following interpretation of this parable of Jesus,
offered recently by a young man from a base community in
Guatemala while visiting a congregation in Iowa. He did not
dismiss the traditional reading of the parable, that those of us
who live a lifetime of Christian discipleship must not resent
those who are welcomed into God's family late in the day, so
to speak. He said that we should welcome them into the family without any resentment, even though that might be difficult. We must not be like the elder brother in the parable of
the prodigal son.

But then he went on to give a brilliant new insight as he
pointed out another dimension to the story. "Think about it,"
he said. "Have you ever had to stand in a marketplace all day,
waiting for someone to offer you work? I can assure you it is
not a good way to spend the day. You hang around, hour after
hour, wondering if you will have any money to buy tomorrow's food for your family. I would rather work through the
heat of the day, knowing that I will receive a day's wage in the
evening, than spend all day worrying about where my family's
food will come from."

"And there's one more thing," he added. "You will note
that the laborers who were employed later in the day did not
know how much they were going to be paid. The owner simply said they would be paid whatever was right. They pre-
sumed that would be less than a day's wage. They did not
know about the pleasant surprise awaiting them. So, even as
they were working, they would still be concerned about
whether they would have enough money for their families."

"Let me tell you," he concluded, "the best way to spend the
day is to work for a boss who is trustworthy and has promised
to pay you."

WORDS FOR MY LIFE

This parable has two lessons for us. The first is the more obvious: We should not resent the blessings of God toward others, even when they seem to exceed the blessings we receive. Even if we were to receive no reward at all for our Christian service, we would have no cause to complain. The privilege and the joy of serving Jesus Christ should be reward enough. We fail to serve Jesus Christ too often for us to be concerned about reward or payment. When did you or I last visit someone in prison or feed someone who was hungry? Whatever we are doing, it is not enough. Our failures in discipleship more than cancel out the times we are faithful. We should be grateful that God does not keep score.

The second lesson, powerfully illustrated by the young man from Guatemala, is that we are not in charge of the vineyard. God is. We are not equals with God but God's creatures. God made us; we did not make God.

One of the most difficult aspects of Christian discipleship today is the acceptance of our creaturely condition. We live in a culture where self-reliance and self-determination are extolled in every walk of life. The possibility that someone else is in charge is not an appealing or comfortable idea for us. Yet the fact of the matter is that God *is* in charge. Whatever God decides to do with us, God is entitled to do.

Instead of complaining about the limitations of our creaturely life (many of which are unrecognized blessings anyway), we should be profoundly grateful that our Creator is the gracious, parental God revealed in Jesus Christ. Ironically, those who are most inconvenienced in life, and especially those who suffer pain or abuse, are most ready to recognize these blessings.

Once we accept our creaturely perspective, we begin to see God as God rather than as the proprietor of a divine convenience store. We begin to realize that the only evaluation we are entitled to make is a self-evaluation of our own discipleship. Let us be thankful that whatever God decides to do with us will be a blessing for us. Let us also be clear that whatever God decides to do with our sisters and brothers of the world will likewise be a blessing for them.

14

The End of Time

Mark 13:1-37

But about that day or hour no one knows, neither the angels in heaven, nor the Son, but only the Father. . . . Therefore, keep awake— for you do not know when the master of the house will come, in the evening, or at midnight, or at cockcrow, or at dawn, or else he may find you asleep when he comes suddenly. And what I say to you I say to all: Keep awake.

Mark 13:32, 35-37

WORDS FOR BIBLE TIMES

The word we use to describe these sayings of Jesus in Mark 13 is *apocalyptic*, from the Greek word meaning "revelation." Apocalyptic writings were a common feature of Jewish thought at the time of Jesus and had two general characteristics: They focused on the end of time, and they made a sharp distinction between the forces of good and evil in the world. In many of these writings we find a vision of the end of the world as a violently destructive event, in which God finally separates the faithful from the unfaithful and creates a new world, free from sin and evil.

Apocalyptic thought influenced the biblical writers. We find this most directly in the books of Daniel and Revelation but also in passages such as this one in Mark's Gospel. The issue the early church faced in considering these writings was how to discern their major emphasis. Indeed, Jesus himself had to face this issue since the writings were part of the tradition he inherited.

As we read through his sayings in Mark 13, it becomes clear that Jesus focused on a message of hope, though he did not abandon the vivid apocalyptic imagery. This world order has to go, and much calamity will occur in the process. But this process will be the birth pangs of a new order, the coming reign of God.

These teachings brought reassurance to the early church. Never mind the turmoils and catastrophes they might have to endure; the word of Jesus was one of hope. God's redemption is at hand. The Son of Man will return to bring God's salvation to fulfillment. Whatever happens, therefore, the disciples and the early church were to remain faithful.

WORDS FOR OUR TIME

As in biblical times, so today we find apocalyptic writings to be a source of strength and comfort when the people of God are facing times of turmoil or persecution. While Christians are facing such times in many places around the world at present, it is difficult for those of us in the Western world to imagine what that is like. So we must be careful how we approach this passage from Mark, and for two reasons.

The first reason is that apocalyptic writings hold a peculiar fascination. They seem to explore the mysteries of eternity. They even seem to unlock some of its secrets. But if we read them carefully—and this passage is a good example—we find frequent warnings not to use them as a blueprint for the future. We are told that the fulfillment of God's promises will come as a total surprise. There is the promise that Christ will return, at which time all the mysteries of human history will be resolved—the mysteries of sin, suffering, pain, oppression, and evil. All accounts will be settled; and God's love, peace, and justice will prevail. But *when* this will happen, and *how* it will happen, we are not told. These secrets remain with God and God alone. Not even the Son of Man will be told the time and the manner of his return.

Therefore we should be less concerned with trying to discern the signs and wonders of the future than with *being ready* for the return of Christ, whenever and however that takes place. Christ's return may come during our lifetime, or we may join the countless others who experience it beyond the grave. But the warning is clear: When it does happen, make sure that Jesus finds us faithfully at work.

The second reason to approach this passage carefully is its context. These sayings were intended to encourage the disciples of Jesus during turmoil and suffering, but we must be careful not to personalize his words. Jesus is not just talking about times of personal suffering, when we feel abandoned or neglected by God. We all experience such times. They come to test us and to make our faith more resilient. But Jesus is talking about those times of real persecution, often accompanied by social and political calamity, when it seems that the whole world is collapsing and that the powers of darkness and evil are winning.

The people of God have weathered such times throughout history, and our own time is no exception. Indeed, the twentieth century has been described as the century of holocausts. The genocides by the Nazis, horrendous though they were, are a small part of the whole. In the former USSR, some forty million people were killed between 1918 and 1953; and in the Maoist revolution in China, some forty-five million died. Right down to the present, humankind continues to wreak havoc on itself all over the planet.

The irony is that those who are in the midst of such chaos and slaughter are more likely to remain faithful than those of us who, from positions of relative comfort and security, find it fascinating to speculate on what these wars and rumors of wars and famines and earthquakes might mean. We had better be careful, very careful indeed, that we do not indulge in such imagining as a way of avoiding our present and immediate Christian obligations.

Let these sayings of Jesus comfort those who are suffering the horrors of wars and persecutions. Let these words convey to them the glorious certainty that the final victory does belong to God. Those of us who are well blessed in this life can also take comfort in this glorious certainty. But let us not become "so heavenly-minded" that we are of no earthly use to Jesus. Let us center our time and our energies on our sisters and brothers who need our help in the midst of their very real calamities, lest Christ return and catch us engaged in idle speculation.

WORDS FOR MY LIFE

"That's all well and good," you might say. "But does this passage have nothing at all to say about the future? Did Jesus say these words only for the benefit of people who were in the midst of suffering and persecution? Are they completely irrelevant for people like myself who live fairly ordinary lives? If they are not meant for everyone, why have they been included in the Bible? If I am not to take these words seriously, how should I take all the other teachings of Jesus?"

The answer to these questions lies in what can best be described as our impatience with God's promises. We keep pestering God to tell us the one thing God is not prepared to let us know—how our salvation is finally going to turn out. Yes, we can expect the predictions of Jesus to come to pass. We can note, for example, that the Temple in Jerusalem was indeed destroyed by the Romans in A.D. 70. And if there is one thing that we can say about the centuries that have intervened since then, it is the regularity of wars, rumors of wars, earthquakes, and famines. We also know that the world is going to end some billions of years into the future—barring some cosmic accident, which is always possible.

The problem with these sayings of Jesus is not with their authenticity but with our wanting to make them cut and dried and to pin them down to a point in time, preferably our time. We should beware of the false prophets, correctly foretold by Jesus, who entice us with their futuristic fascinations. They thoroughly misunderstand the purpose of these warnings, which are not given so that we might calculate the future but rather to reassure us that, *whatever* happens, God will take care of us.

In the meantime, we are to be faithful, knowing that nothing—no war, no rumor of war, no famine, no cosmic disaster, nothing in the present, nothing yet to come, nothing in the whole of creation—can separate us from the parental love of God (Romans 8:38-39). Nothing. Nothing at all.

15

A Woman's Extravagance
Mark 14:3-9

But Jesus said, "Let her alone; why do you
trouble her? She has performed a good service
for me. For you always have the poor with
you, and you can show kindness to them
whenever you wish; but you will not always
have me."

Mark 14:6-7

WORDS FOR BIBLE TIMES

The story in Mark 14:3-9 has several interesting aspects.
In the first place, Mark identifies the host, something
that we rarely find elsewhere in this Gospel. Most of the time
we are informed only that Jesus is the guest in someone's
home. Then we are told that the host is a leper. Whether or
not his leprosy has been cured, this is a household that has
known the religious and social disgrace of the disease. Jesus is
making an important statement by being there at all. As the
home of a leper, this was probably a humble dwelling, due to
the difficulty the family must have had in making ends meet
over the years. Indeed, this may well have encouraged the
general disapproval of the woman's use of expensive oint-
ment on Jesus.

It is also interesting that the woman herself is not identified. A later tradition has linked her with Mary Magdalene,
but nothing in the passage warrants such an identification. In
fact, the anonymity of the woman is a critical dimension of
the story because it serves as a model for the women we find

in the Bible—or rather, for the women we do not find in the Bible. We know they were there, but they are rarely mentioned explicitly. And when we do meet them by name, we often have to read between the lines to flesh out who they were and what they did.

This area of biblical research is sometimes viewed as inappropriate, since it seems to be putting things into the Scriptures that are not there. However, if we believe that the biblical writers are telling us about real people, living out their faith in the real world, then the role of women is greatly understated in the Bible. So the task of giving them their due place in Christian tradition can be an exciting journey of discovery. Once we start searching the Scriptures with this task in mind, we find that Jesus was far more open to women and far more sensitive to their concerns than other rabbis were. And the women who associated with Jesus were often far more sensitive to the nature of his ministry and mission than the male disciples were.

This story is a good illustration. The woman's very presence in the room would have been unusual, for women did not eat with men. It is all the more significant, therefore, that Jesus gives her an identity if not a name. While others talk about her and judge her, Jesus declares that she, of all the people in the room, has the clearest understanding of who he is and of what lies ahead. The communication between the two of them must have been electric.

WORDS FOR OUR TIME

The world is still a place of contrasts, just as it was in Jesus' day. Despite the amazing progress in human knowledge worldwide, the rich are still getting richer and the poor are sliding further into poverty. We now have the technology to feed all the people in the world, yet five hundred million human beings are hungry every day and fifty thousand still die every day from hunger or hunger-related diseases. We have now seen planet earth photographed from outer space, making us the first generation of human beings to see that we are indeed a global community. Yet there are as many refugees today as ever there have been. Even in the United States of America, the wealthiest nation in human history, the number of home-less people continues to rise.

The self-justifying arguments have not changed either. We still hear people say that the poor should "learn to help them-selves" and that "poverty will always be a problem." In a political cartoon at the time of an economic summit in Mex-ico some years ago, a peasant is looking up at the veranda of a mansion, from which a Western tourist is looking down. The peasant is asking, "But señor, what are bootstraps?"

As our Christian sisters and brothers in disadvantaged countries tirelessly point out to us, the issue is not whether people are willing to work for their own food but whether they are allowed access to the land to grow their food. Eco-nomic injustice is the scandal of the modern world; and as long as we do not attend to it, we offend the God of right-eousness and incur God's wrath.

Why, then, does Jesus rebuke his disciples for scolding this woman? Surely they have a point, and a good one. Even if we concede that only the best is good enough for God, why did Jesus say that we will always have the poor? Could he mean that God intends some people to live in poverty, so that wealthy people like ourselves can acquire charitable disposi-tions—a means of grace by default? If so, then we might as well accept that the world will never change and devote our time and talents to preparing for eternity, where the poor will of course also get their reward.

Even a cursory glance through the Scriptures tells us that this is not what Jesus meant. Of course, some people choose poverty as a lifestyle in order to reject their culture. But a great deal of poverty throughout the world is due to ignorance and bigotry, not least of which is religious bigotry. But a great deal of poverty and hunger is due to the exploitation of disad-vantaged nations by advantaged nations, and the teaching of Jesus makes clear that God will hold this sin to our charge.

The point Jesus is making is that the sin, disease, evil, and hunger of the world are not going to be healed overnight. However faithfully his disciples work at their task, it is going to take time. And while the parental love of God will ulti-mately prevail on earth as in heaven, the first disciples, and those of us who have followed them, will always have the poor with us in a very real sense. Jesus is not advocating a principle here but merely making an observation.

Jesus is also making clear to the disciples that, because of the extended nature of their task, they will have to sustain their communion with him. This can happen only if they worship him as the Anointed One of God. Only through spiritual union with Christ can they receive the grace and the power to live out his teachings in the world. The woman understood this truth far more clearly and instinctively than the men did. Jesus rightly foretold that her act would become a permanent part of the gospel.

The poor are with us today, and they will be with us tomorrow. We must not rest until their suffering is alleviated and all human beings have the dignity of work and the freedom to support themselves and their children. But as we undertake this task, we must worship the One who instructs us and empowers us, until every tear is dried and every wound healed.

WORDS FOR MY LIFE

At this point, we might be forgiven for heaving a huge sigh of relief. "Well, at least we don't have to change the world overnight. Thank goodness for that." But a moment's reflection tells us that this cannot be our response. When we do worship Jesus in spirit and in truth, his teachings confront us. This woman at Bethany created a sacred space for Jesus to be worshiped, but we must never forget that this is also the rabbi who expects us to do what he tells us to do.

Jesus understands our limitations, both of time and of resources, and also knows our profound need of grace. But Jesus still expects us to do our best with what we have been given. Perhaps you are already tithing your income and your time to your church. Would it seriously hurt you to give more? The United States of America has a great opportunity to help the poor of the world. What are we doing to influence our national leaders to seize this opportunity?

As we worship Jesus, this week and every week, remember the act of this woman. Precisely because he is the Anointed One of God, the Messiah, the Christ, we must obey his instructions. We must feed the poor.

16

Understanding God's Law of Love

Luke 6:37-42

Do not judge, and you will not be judged; do not condemn, and you will not be condemned. Forgive, and you will be forgiven; give, and it will be given to you.

Luke 6:37-38

WORDS FOR BIBLE TIMES

In Luke 6:37-42 Jesus gives us the very essence of his teachings—the fulfillment of the Law, the Jewish Torah. As we noted in Lesson 10, the Torah was given to the Hebrews as confirmation of their covenant with God, a binding agreement in which God undertook to be their God and they in turn agreed to be God's people.

The history of this covenant relationship was marked on one hand by the complete reliability and faithfulness of God and on the other hand by the repeated waywardness and infidelity of the Hebrews. So often did this happen that the prophet Jeremiah envisioned a day when God would make a new covenant with the people of Israel and Judah, a covenant marked by the indwelling presence of God in each person's heart. No one would need admonition or instruction in the Law because everyone would be completely of one mind with God, from the least to the greatest (Jeremiah 31:31-34).

This was the covenant relationship that Jesus inaugurated—the new covenant, the fulfillment of the Torah. It was also the very issue over which he was taken to task by the rabbinical teachers of his time. Their anger was deep-rooted, for they were guardians of a tradition that went all the way back to Abraham and Moses. The Torah had come to have particular significance, however, in the centuries since the Babylonian exile of the Jews. During those traumatic years in the sixth century B.C., the Law had been carefully preserved, then painstakingly compiled and edited by the community of people who returned to Judah after the Exile. It was rightly revered, for it was the core of their identity as God's people.

Unfortunately, in their concern to keep the Torah at the center of their religious and civic life, the rabbis had allowed it to become more important than the covenant relationship with God that it represented. The living tradition had become traditionalism. The covenant with God no longer shaped their understanding of the Torah; the Torah had come to shape their understanding of the covenant.

Jesus was concerned to reverse these priorities and to make the Torah contingent once again on the covenant relationship with God. This concern of Jesus in no way devalued the Torah, but it shifted the emphasis away from a set of codified laws and toward the God whose basic nature was parental concern.

Against this background of shift in emphasis, the teaching of Jesus takes on a childlike simplicity: There can be no judgment of another person in light of God's law of love, because the Law itself can never substitute for God.

WORDS FOR OUR TIME

However, this understanding leaves us with a critical question. What about the laws that are needed by society for the day-to-day ordering of life? Surely we cannot avoid passing judgment on criminal behavior. What about human justice at a practical level?

This is an important question; and to answer it, we must take one step back from the biblical setting. In the history of the Hebrews, the Torah was a unique blend of religious teaching and social legislation. It combined their covenant with God and the regulation of their nation as God's people.

Christian history, on the other hand, has been more checkered. At various times and places theocracies—systems of government where God, or God's religious representatives, have been the final authority—have governed nations. At other times the church has held considerable political power, especially in the Western world.

For the most part, however, the Christian law of love has not prevailed at national levels. Human laws have functioned alongside rather than under religious authority, and in the United States of America the distinction between the two has been quite explicit.

Interestingly, while the Torah did not make this distinction between government and religion, the Jews encountered it in the form of the Roman law by which they were also governed at the time of Jesus. He himself made that clear when the Pharisees tried to trap him over the question of whether or not they should pay taxes to the emperor (Matthew 22:15-22).

Christian disciples, therefore, have usually had two sets of laws by which to abide—those of their community and nation and the law of love as taught by Jesus Christ. Compliance with human law usually presents little difficulty, since this law is primarily concerned with the minimal ordering of society. Even so, at times Christ's law of love must take precedence over human laws. When human laws are inconsistent with God's parental concern for humanity, Christians may have to challenge or even disobey them. So it was with the early Christians over pagan worship in the Roman Empire. So it was with nineteenth-century Christians in the United States over slavery. So it was with German Christians in the 1930's under Adolf Hitler. And so it may well be in our own day and age.

Such conditions place Christian disciples in a number of tensions—tensions that are often difficult to discern because they come so well disguised. There is the tension of witnessing to God's law of love in a world that is not yet ready for the coming reign of God. This tension in turn leads to the tension of determining which of our human laws we can obey in good conscience, which of them we must challenge in light of God's law of love, and which of them are merely the inconveniences of living in a sinful world. We even find tensions in our Christian relationships, for the benefits of life in God's household do not excuse us from wrestling against our own residual sin as well as against the sin of the world.

In short, we find living according to God's law of love and witnessing to it in the world to be very hard work. There are no easy answers, and there are no shortcuts. We have to draw on every one of our gifts and graces, including our reason and our integrity.

Accordingly, our primary task in the midst of these tensions must be the embodiment of the law of love in God's household. We must make it the measure of all that we think and say and do as the children of God; for it is nothing less than the law of all eternity, the kingdom of God on earth as in heaven.

We must also live out this law of love beyond the church. The rules of God's household may not yet prevail throughout the world, and the human laws that we need in the meantime may require us to make judgments and impose penalties that are fraught with human imperfections; but Christ's teaching must still be our watchword. Whatever judgment we have to make on other people's behavior, we must never presume to judge their hearts. That remains God's prerogative. The only heart we can even attempt to judge is our own. And that kind of judgment will quickly make us aware of our need to forgive rather than to condemn. We must do this seventy-seven times, or seventy times seven if need be, so that we ourselves can repent, be forgiven, and be reconciled to God.

WORDS FOR MY LIFE

The most important aspect of these teachings of Jesus is what they have to say about personal discipleship. The key is in Luke 6:40: "A disciple is not above the teacher, but everyone who is fully qualified will be like the teacher."

Jesus understood that the greatest pitfall his disciples faced would be the intimacy of their relationship with him. Having sacrificed so much to follow him, they would be tempted to assume that they had the inside track with Jesus, so to speak, and to become possessive of their discipleship. Indeed, James and John went so far as to ask for the privilege of sitting on either side of Jesus in eternity, though they did at least let their mother make the request.

Jesus gently pointed out that the kingdom of heaven included no such privileges. The only privilege was that of sacrificial service (Matthew 20:20-23).

Possessiveness in relationships stems from insecurity, and insecure people will quickly judge others in order to feel more secure themselves. It is a vicious circle, and Jesus makes clear in these parables that he wants none of it. Christ, and Christ alone, will be the judge of any disciple; because Christ, and Christ alone, is the teacher. Christ will determine the potential of each one of us, and Christ will evaluate our faithfulness.

Thus, it is not only inappropriate but downright foolish to judge anyone else's discipleship. The humor of the blind leading the blind might be expressed today as a thrice-divorced marriage counselor, or a chain-smoking lung specialist—someone whose evaluative and leadership skills are clearly in question. The teaching is plain and simple: No one has the inside track with Jesus.

17

How Long Is God Willing to Wait?

Luke 13:1-17

He replied, "Sir, let it alone for one more year, until I dig around it and put manure on it. If it bears fruit next year, well and good; but if not, you can cut it down."

Luke 13:8-9

WORDS FOR BIBLE TIMES

Luke 13:1-17 includes one of the thorniest aspects of Jesus' teachings in the parable of the fig tree. Elsewhere in the Gospels Jesus tells us that God is loving and parental and wants us all back home where we belong. He does, of course, make clear that the invitation is not cheap. The only way for us to come home is to repent of our sins and to be forgiven. Only then can we be reconciled to live in God's household. But even so, the invitation is extended to everyone; and if God is as loving as Jesus tells us, then we might surely assume that God, like any human mother or father, will wait for us all to come, however long it takes.

Yet here in this parable we are told that the longer we postpone our repentance, the more we bring things down on our own heads. The teachings evident in this parable are blunt, if not brutal: Unrepentant sinners can expect to perish, just like the Galileans slaughtered by Pilate and the eighteen who were killed in Jerusalem when the tower of Siloam fell on them.

Later in the chapter, the point is made even more directly: Some people will be admitted to God's household, and some will be thrown out. "Indeed, some are last who will be first, and some are first who will be last" (13:28-30).

What are we to make of these apparent contradictions? Those of us who are parents can readily imagine throwing rebellious children out of the house when we have reached the end of our tether. Maybe some of us have done so. But few of us would not immediately relent if those same children changed their ways and asked to come back home. If this is true of us as human parents, then can we not expect as much, if not more, from God?

This seems to be the message of the parable of the fig tree (13:6-9). As we have noted in earlier lessons, the parables of Jesus are stories intended to make one point, and the point of this parable is not the lack of fruit on the tree. Rather, the point is the readiness of the owner of the vineyard to let the gardener give it another chance to bear fruit, even to spend some extra time giving it special care.

From this perspective, we might see the dire warnings of Jesus not as God's last word but as the threats of a loving parent trying to tell disobedient and thoughtless children that they are in deep trouble. It is not a question of what God will do to them but of what they will do to themselves if they fail to heed the warnings. And if the only way to get through to these headstrong children is to let them experience some of the consequences of their behavior, that too will have to happen. Though even then, God, the infinitely loving parent, will always be forgiving when they come to their senses.

The same point is made in a different way when Jesus heals the crippled woman (13:10-17). The woman had been ill for eighteen years, and Jesus cured her on the sabbath. When the leader of the synagogue, whose understanding of the Torah was legalistic rather than covenantal, criticized Jesus before the crowd, Jesus rebuked him and explained to him that the letter of the Law can never be the issue. The Law is to bring people back into God's family, not to keep them out.

If anyone should have known this, a leader of the synagogue should have. The history of the Jews had shown time and again that God dispenses justice, and the prophets had repeatedly emphasized that God's justice has a pronounced bias toward mercy. Likewise, God determines the purpose of the Law, which is never to be interpreted as a freestanding institution. The Torah was given in lovingkindness to shape the covenant relationship between God and the Jews. Otherwise they could never have broken it so many times and been forgiven. A leader of the synagogue should have known that as well. No wonder he was shamed into silence by a jubilant crowd.

Mercy such as this, added Rabbi Jesus, will spread throughout the earth as the kingdom of heaven is fulfilled. There may not be much of it around for the present, but it will ultimately be explosive in its impact on the world.

WORDS FOR OUR TIME

The problem with the rabbinical teachers at the time of Jesus was that they wanted things cut and dried, just as we do today. Instead of reaching out to stubborn sinners with God's message of mercy, all too often those of us who already belong to the household of faith want to know what God is going to do to punish them. Indeed, that was the very next question for Jesus: In Jerusalem someone asked, "Lord, will only a few be saved?" (13:23)

The question, of course, entirely misses the point of Jesus' message. The teachings of Jesus are never concerned with how many are to be saved. Rather, they are concerned with how long God is willing to wait and how far God is willing to go to bring the whole of this wayward human family back home.

Yes, Jesus gave dire warnings about sinners who reject God's grace. But the fact that he gave these warnings almost two thousand years ago tells us that they were not for any particular time in history but for all time and for all eternity. The consequences of disobeying God will always be disastrous, now and in eternity. Likewise, the parental love of God will always be God's last word, now and in eternity.

Some people take these dire warnings of Jesus to mean that if people reject the saving grace of Jesus Christ in this life, they can expect damnation, or something very nasty, beyond the grave. They argue that any idea of forgiveness in eternity merely gives people permission to live recklessly here on earth and thereby makes the warnings of Jesus redundant. But this is the same attitude that the leader in the synagogue had; he could see the Torah only in legalistic terms. Nothing that Jesus said or did can ever be interpreted legalistically, especially when it concerns eternity.

The teachings of Jesus ultimately declare only one thing—that God's parental concern to have us all back home is limitless. As we have noted, the invitation is not cheap. In fact, it cost the Son of God his life. But precisely because God pleads with us from the cross, we know that legalistic time limits are not the issue. God will scan the horizon for returning prodigal children for as long as it takes, now and in eternity.

WORDS FOR MY LIFE

One of the most difficult tasks for a Christian is learning how to be patient with people who ignore or reject the gospel of Jesus Christ. Many Christians do not have this difficulty, quite simply because they sense no urgency about repentance for sins, their own or other people's. One of the most corrupting aspects of our culture today is the willingness to overlook one another's offenses if shallow cordiality can work to our mutual advantage; and all too often this becomes our attitude toward God as well.

Those of us who do understand the urgency of repentance and forgiveness, however, are frustrated when we expend time and energy sharing the gospel of Jesus Christ only to have our efforts spurned. These feelings are even more understandable when we see the continued suffering of the world due to unrepentant sinners who hold the reins of worldly power. We become impatient to see the final outcome of God's salvation. We want to see a world in which the sinners are called to account and the pain and the anguish of the sinned-against are brought to an end.

If we are not careful, this frustration can seriously damage our own relationship with Jesus Christ. Any hardening of our hearts, any cynicism about the seemingly endless delay in the fulfillment of God's promises, will distance us from Jesus

Christ. There is only one sure way to avoid these feelings of frustration, and that is to look on the whole world as God's family—the sinned-against *and* the sinners. God's purpose is to bring them all back home, every single one of them; and the question is never "How many?" but always "How long?"

We should note that the parable of the fig tree is set in a vineyard. In the Scripture the vineyard is often a symbol for Israel, which means that the fig tree refers to those who are already God's people. As Christ's disciples, we should take this setting to heart.

The urgency of our task is to bring the sufferings of Christ's little ones to an end as soon as possible. To the extent that we neglect these little ones, we risk being cut down. To the extent that we feed them, clothe them, and love them, we bear fruit in the vineyard. We really have no time to think of anything else, least of all how all the other trees in the vineyard are doing.

18
The Word Made Flesh
John 1:1-18

In the beginning was the Word, and the Word was with God, and the Word was God.

· ·

And the Word became flesh and lived among us, and we have seen his glory, the glory as of a father's only son, full of grace and truth.

John 1:1, 14

WORDS FOR BIBLE TIMES

These verses (John 1:1-18) are known as the Prologue to the Gospel of John, and they make clear that the central theme of what follows will be the person of Jesus. The writer had good reasons for taking such an approach. By the time this Gospel appeared, which scholars generally agree was in the closing years of the first century, the immediacy of Christ's return was less of an issue than his identity. If he had claimed to be uniquely related to God, and if he had been raised from the dead, and if he was indeed the mediator of a new covenant with God, then all of this had to be given some meaning, pending his return.

The messianic tradition of the Hebrews could explain only so much, because Jesus had not been the kind of Messiah they had expected. This Messiah had fulfilled the promises of God in unexpected ways. Moreover, as the apostle Paul had established in confrontation with the Jerusalem church, the Kingdom that Jesus had inaugurated was for all the world (Galatians 2:11-21). It was for Gentiles no less than Jews. Jesus had not only fulfilled the Torah; he had extended God's covenant to all of humanity.

We now have a new age, a new order, in which "There is no longer Jew or Greek, there is no longer slave or free, there is no longer male and female; for all of you are one in Christ Jesus" (3:28). The early church knew that Jesus had to be understood as more than the Jewish Messiah if this good news was to reach all people and to the ends of the earth.

The writer of this Gospel, in all probability the disciple John, the son of Zebedee, had no doubt that the astounding claims of this young rabbi from Nazareth were profoundly true. The question was, How could he make these claims understandable to people who were not in the Hebrew tradition as well as to those who were?

To do this, John described Jesus as "The Word," a term that had meaning for Jews and Gentiles alike. For the Jews, "the word of God" was understood as communication from God and was in fact the closest that the Hebrew Scriptures came to a description of God. The Gentiles would have known that Greek philosophy had formed a concept of the "Word" (*Logos*) as the creative and sustaining spirit of God in the world. Indeed, Philo of Alexandria, a first-century Jewish scholar trained in Greek philosophy, had gone so far as to identify the *Logos* as God's creative agent in the world.

So John's language carried immediate meaning for his contemporaries as well as lasting significance for the church. The Word, the *Logos*, is the young rabbi from Nazareth. Time and eternity are fused in a moment of history. God becomes one of us.

WORDS FOR OUR TIME

The most powerful phrase in this prologue comes in John 1:14: "The Word became flesh." God became a human being at a particular time and place in human history. That is our starting point if we are to make the gospel meaningful in the increasingly secular and pagan world of today.

First of all, we don't have to make this truth any more complicated than it really is. Theologians explore it in technical depth because such explorations are vital and necessary for the ongoing tradition of the church. But technical theology need not concern us in our daily Christian living, any more than we need to understand principles of composition and counterpoint to appreciate a Beethoven symphony or to understand the principles of aerodynamics and turbojet engines to travel in a jetliner. The fact of the matter is that God is God and that every creature of God knows this instinctively, especially human beings.

Yet no one has seen God, and this presents Christians with two powerful challenges from a sinful world. The first challenge comes from those who reject the existence of God outright. After all, they argue, where is the proof? No one has had a clear sighting of God. Besides, those who accept the reality of God seem to have it no better and no worse in life than everyone else. Would it not be better, then, to leave the whole question open? This might make believers a little less secure, but it is far better to have believers less secure than to have them force their opinions on the rest of us. The world has enough bigotry without adding any more in the name of Jesus Christ.

The second challenge is more subtle. It comes from those who do believe in God but who then proceed to create the kind of god that offers them maximum benefits with minimum obligations, a vague divine presence that gives soothing answers to troublesome questions. Once again, in the absence of any clear sighting of God, are we not entitled to our own ideas?

That is why John 1:14 is the punch line of the whole Bible. In Jesus of Nazareth, we *do* have a clear sighting of God. This human being, born in Bethlehem and raised in Nazareth, was a revelation of almighty God in a form that ordinary human beings could understand. To see God suddenly, and in full glory, would be more than we could stand. But in Jesus of Nazareth—a good, wise, and compassionate teacher and friend—we see that the God who created the universe is also God our Savior.

Of course, we cannot explain these truths any more than

we can explain a beautiful sunset or a starlit night sky. That is why Jesus told us to seek for childlike simplicity and wonder if we want to enter the kingdom of heaven (Matthew 18:3-4; Luke 18:17).

A five-year-old girl convinced me of this one Sunday during a children's sermon. I had asked, "How do we know there is a God?" and I shall never forget her answer: "Because you just *know!*"

WORDS FOR MY LIFE

Even so, the nonbelievers still have a point. If God is really the loving, parental God that Jesus revealed to us, why are we left with so many questions? Why is the revelation incomplete? Jesus may have been the light of the world, but here we are two thousand years later with little to show for it except his promise that one day the kingdom of God will come on earth as in heaven. In the meantime, you and I must be patient and faithful; we must place our childlike trust in God. In moments of doubt or crisis, however, that is easier to talk about than it is to do. Could God be playing games with us? Why the riddles? Why not come clean and show us more clearly the things of eternity?

The answer to our questions lies in John's description of Jesus as the light of the world (John 1:9; 8:12). Light reveals what has previously been hidden by darkness, and this is precisely what Jesus does for us. In Jesus of Nazareth we not only have a sighting of God, but we also have an exposure of who we are—sinful human beings, whose nature is deeply flawed. As sinners, we cannot understand the things of God—at least, not yet.

On both counts, we have been told the truth—the truth about God and the truth about ourselves. The God who was in Christ is willing, indeed longing, to give us boundless blessings. But we cannot receive these blessings, because the truth about ourselves is that we are lost. We are part of a planet that has gone seriously astray from its Creator. We might speculate endlessly on how and why this happened, but the light that comes from Jesus Christ shows us that there is no way to deny it. The amazing thing is that the loving, parental

God who created us has taken a dramatic and dangerous initiative to save us. The God who created the universe has assumed human form in order to invite us back home.

Whenever we find this truth difficult to accept, it is because we are blind to everything except our own self-interest. We are unwilling to give up our sinful conveniences—the convenience of ignoring God altogether, the convenience of lip service to a god who does not challenge our selfish ways.

The God of the universe, however, is not willing to leave things the way they are. This God will not leave us alone. The God who was in Christ went to the cross to bring us back home. The only question is whether we will accept the invitation gracefully, or whether we will put ourselves through the inconvenience, the grief, and (if we are determined to be stubborn) the torment of useless resistance.

In reality we all are God's wayward children, and God yearns to have us back home where we belong. How do we know this? Jesus of Nazareth, God in person, said so.

19

Receiving the Holy Spirit
Acts 2:1-12

And suddenly from heaven there came a sound like the rush of a violent wind, and it filled the entire house where they were sitting. Divided tongues, as of fire, appeared among them, and a tongue rested on each of them. All of them were filled with the Holy Spirit and began to speak in other languages, as the Spirit gave them ability.

Acts 2:2-4

WORDS FOR BIBLE TIMES

The dramatic events in Acts 2:1-12 introduce us to the third person of the Trinity, the God who is three in one. The experience of the apostles at Pentecost was more than a spiritual sensation. It was a baptism, a pouring out of God's Spirit in a new way. It had been envisioned by the prophet Joel (Joel 2:28-29), foretold by John the Baptist (Matthew 3:11), and promised by Jesus himself after his resurrection (Acts 1:5). Most important, it was a pouring out of God's Spirit with a purpose—to give the apostles the power and the gifts to witness to Jesus Christ "to the ends of the earth" (1:8).

Whatever words the apostles used to describe it, this was a breathtaking event. It was a powerful reassurance of the life and teachings of Jesus, and it gave new meaning to his death and resurrection. As Jesus had promised, this "Advocate," this "Spirit of truth," had indeed come to abide with them (John

14:16-17), but in a way that far exceeded their expectations. This baptism was a whole new revelation of the love and the power of God, a mystical union with the divine. No wonder they seemed drunk.

The outpouring of the Holy Spirit at Pentecost brought a gift that would be the mark of the church's mission to the world—the gift of communication with those who spoke different languages. Persons have attempted to provide practical explanations for this spiritual phenomenon. Possibly everyone in the crowd understood a smattering of Greek or Aramaic and was able to follow the gist of what the apostles were saying. Or the apostles may have known some key phrases in various languages due to the amount of foreign traffic passing through Palestine.

But this is clearly not how the apostles themselves viewed their empowerment. They saw it as a uniquely spiritual blessing, and the occurrence of the same phenomenon at other times and places in the early church indicates that the apostles were probably exercising the gift of "speaking in tongues," a form of ecstatic utterance that did not conform with any known language.

Undoubtedly, the purpose of the gift was missional. It allowed the apostles to witness to people from many different places without any language barriers.

WORDS FOR OUR TIME

The difficulty with this passage for many Christians today is not what happened on the day of Pentecost. The story gives us the sense that something quite wonderful and miraculous took place due to the empowerment of Christ's resurrection, and few Christians find that hard to believe. Of course, the apostles were deliriously happy, given all that had happened.

The difficulty with the passage stems rather from how the church of today should acknowledge and receive the Holy Spirit, the person of the triune God who is probably the least understood and arguably the most abused. The problem is that we are reluctant to forgo our own ideas about God. We find the revelation at Pentecost too disturbing, so we cling to an idea of God that seems to be simpler—a God we can envisage without having to deal with this person or that. In other words, we wish to control our relationship with God, and that is precisely what the Holy Spirit denies us.

Once we see the sinfulness of such a desire, we can begin to appreciate the richness of a Trinity who is indeed one God but who is also three persons with three identities, three forms, three roles, and most important of all, three kinds of presence. It is all well and good to believe in one God as the Creator of the universe, but we can easily turn this divine Creator into a vague heavenly presence rather like "The Force" of the *Star Wars* movies. Such a God can be conveniently consigned to heaven, available on call when required, but otherwise leaving us to our own devices here on earth—devices that eventually land us in all kinds of trouble.

If we accept that God is more than a vague heavenly presence, however, things change quite radically. Not only do we have the God who is the awesome Creator of the universe, but we also have the God who was Jesus of Nazareth, the divine human being. This second person of the Trinity, the Son of God, tells us that God is keenly interested in this planet and everything that lives on it, sufficiently interested to take part in our earthly existence to save us from self-destruction. This Nazarene is also our God—God our Savior, God in the power of human flesh.

God is also the sympathetic, ever-present Spirit, whose business is to be our constant companion and guide. This third person of the Trinity inspires us, empowers us, corrects us, and above all, comforts us. The Holy Spirit is the God who is always available and from whom it is impossible to get away.

In short, the message of Pentecost is that God is our family in the deepest sense of the word—our Creator and our parent, our Savior and our sibling, and also our most intimate friend and companion.

WORDS FOR MY LIFE

The experience of the apostles at Pentecost was so dramatic that it presents us with a pitfall. Given their baptism of fire, we are inclined to identify the Holy Spirit primarily with powerful sensations. When this happens, we tend to overlook all the other ways we receive and experience the Holy Spirit, thereby limiting our knowledge of this person of the Trinity to the most expressive and emotional of our spiritual gifts.

To avoid this pitfall, we must remember that, even though the apostles experienced this person of the triune God in a new and powerful way at Pentecost, the Holy Spirit is the same God they had known all along. This is the God they saw revealed in Jesus Christ, the God who brought their forebears out of slavery in Egypt, the God who made the world and everything in it. This Pentecostal baptism was memorable, but it was by no means an exclusive encounter with the Spirit of God.

The Holy Spirit is the God who is worshiped week by week in all our churches, who graced us when we were baptized into the faith, and who has been watching over us with parental care all our lives. Most important of all, this is the same God who died for us on the cross.

We must remember that the three persons of the Trinity are not separate; they are one and the same God. The Holy Spirit is the person of God who makes God *personal*—to you, to me, and to everyone who is privileged to know the God who was in Christ. Jesus promised his disciples nothing less— that the Holy Spirit would come to abide with them and in them (John 14:15-17, 25-26). Jesus promised that through the work of the Holy Spirit the world would remember his teachings and experience his love and peace and justice.

If you are not sure whether you have the Holy Spirit in your life, you should not plague yourself with doubts. Rather, you should ask whether you know in your heart that Jesus is the Son of God, the Savior of the world. Ask whether you know that his teachings are true. Ask whether you trust in his prayer,

"Your kingdom come.

Your will be done,

on earth as it is in heaven" (Matthew 6:10).

If your answer to these questions is yes, then you *have* been baptized with the Holy Spirit. Your baptism may not have been as dramatic as on the day of Pentecost; but how you received the Holy Spirit matters far less than knowing, here and now, that the Spirit of God, the Spirit of Christ, is dwelling in your heart.

20

Discipleship and Marriage
1 Corinthians 7:10-16

It is to peace that God has called you. Wife, for all you know, you might save your husband. Husband, for all you know, you might save your wife.

1 Corinthians 7:15-16

WORDS FOR BIBLE TIMES

Throughout this letter Paul is dealing with a contentious group of Christians at Corinth. Rather than go into the deeper questions of the gospel and thereby give them further opportunity for disagreement, he writes to them on practical issues of faith and Christian living. This passage is an excellent example. In light of the teachings of Jesus and of the Torah, what are the guidelines for Christian marriage?

Paul's answers to this and other questions show us the importance of right teaching in the early church. The gospel Paul had proclaimed to the Corinthians carried the promise of eternal life in the power of Christ's resurrection. This of course meant the reconsideration and even the rejection of many worldly values. The question was, Which worldly values should be rejected, and which should remain in place, pending the return of Christ and the fulfillment of the coming reign of God?

The social and spiritual issues of marriage assumed an important place on this agenda. Whether believers should marry nonbelievers was the obvious question. Whether a woman or man who converted to the Christian faith should remain married to a husband or wife who did not convert was a more difficult question. Since Paul wrote this letter in the firm belief that the fulfillment of the reign of God was imminent, his advice on these issues is deeply spiritual. At the same time, his words are realistic, reflecting the possibility that he himself was married or widowed. This would not be surprising, since it was normal for Jewish rabbis to be married.

WORDS FOR OUR TIME

Paul's teachings confront us at a time when sustaining a faithful Christian marriage is not easy. The very institution, especially in the Western world, is undergoing some radical changes. On one hand, people today have significant new freedoms. Young couples do not have to contend with parental control or interference to nearly the same extent previous generations did. Age, religion, and race are no longer the barriers they once were; and women are rejecting any marital role that implies subjection or inferiority as they assume greater self-confidence in society at large.

On the other hand, the changes are bringing some mixed blessings. The most conspicuous of these is the sharp rise in divorce. In many instances, this represents a hard-won freedom, most especially for those women who, through countless generations, have been trapped in abusive relationships by social and religious discrimination. Yet abuse is not the issue in many divorces, and the frequency of remarriage is eroding the meaning of the wedding vow "until we are parted by death." People from polygamous cultures dryly observe that those of us in the West, while officially condemning polygamy, merely practice it progressively.

The climate of uncertainty generated by these changes makes it imperative that Christians of today understand and practice marriage in light of the teachings of Jesus. Marriage remains the most intimate of human relationships—more intimate than that of friends, sisters, and brothers, more intimate even than that of parents and children. For in marriage the love that binds two people together is immeasurably deepened through physical union. Two human bodies become one, and in so doing they surrender themselves completely to each other. In the traditional wedding litany, not often used today, the bride and the groom say to each other, "With my body, I thee worship." Marriage is that deep and that sacred.

It follows, therefore, that if our most intimate spiritual relationship is with God, through Jesus Christ and in the presence of the Holy Spirit, then for a Christian to wed someone who does not have this same intimacy with God is bound to create a barrier or chasm in the marriage. This is why the Corinthians asked such questions of Paul. It was not a matter of religious observance or social custom but of common sense and candor, qualities that any couple should reasonably expect from each other in a marriage of love, dignity, and mutual freedom.

WORDS FOR MY LIFE

Nowhere do we find the rich mysteries of the Trinity, the God who is three in one, more meaningfully expressed than in the dynamics of a Christian marriage.

Our first reaction may be to question this observation, because there appear to be contradictions in associating a marriage so closely with a trinitarian God. For example, how do married couples relate to a God who is parental? Will they not feel the same sense of intrusion they feel from interfering parents or parents-in-law? Will the intrusion not be compounded when they try to relate to Jesus Christ? As a young man once expressed it during marriage counseling, "I'm having a hard job making room for Jesus in our relationship. To tell you the truth, I'm jealous."

The third person of the Trinity removes these intrusions, making a Christian marriage not only the deep union of two human beings but also a deep union with God. In and through the Holy Spirit, the couple's love for each other does not detract from their relationship with God, nor does God intrude on their times of deepest intimacy. The Holy Spirit communes with them and makes their love even more exquisite. Their oneness finds deeper expression emotionally, spiritually, and physically. In a Christian marriage the Holy Spirit makes the physical union unspeakably beautiful.

In turn, the Holy Spirit opens a Christian marriage to the teachings of Jesus Christ. Discipleship becomes increasingly exacting as Christians grow in grace; and if marriage partners are not mutually committed to Christ, each will resent the demands that Jesus makes on the other. The presence of the Holy Spirit in a marriage grants the freedom to be obedient to Christ without any such resentment.

So the words of Paul are as relevant today as they were for the Corinthians. If you are a Christian disciple, you should not consider marrying a person who does not have the same commitment to Christ. If you do, one of the relationships will be seriously impaired, the relationship with your spouse or the relationship with Christ. For the same reason, if you are already married when you make your commitment to Christ and your spouse does not join in that commitment, your marriage will lack spiritual intimacy. However, this does not mean that you should separate or divorce (unless your spouse leaves you or becomes abusive); because if your spouse does not sabotage your discipleship, you are well placed to be a powerful means of grace for him or her. You have the opportunity to witness to Christ in the most sensitive of situations— living with someone who knows you well enough to discern God's grace in your life.

This still leaves us with what is possibly the most troublesome teaching in the passage. It is made all the more difficult because Paul cites Jesus on the issue (Mark 10:11-12; Luke 16:18): If a Christian couple should find it necessary to separate or divorce, remarriage is out of the question, except to the original partner. Are we to take Jesus at his word on this? Is a Christian who has divorced and married someone else really living in adultery?

The teaching may be difficult, but it may also be the one we should take most seriously. At a time when personal fulfillment rather than faithful discipleship seems to be the ultimate measure of a Christian marriage, Paul reverses the priority. Precisely because the reign of God is imminent, our marital relationships are far less important than our faithful service to Jesus Christ. Accordingly, Christians should separate or divorce only if their discipleship is in jeopardy. If they do so for any other reason, then in light of the marriage vows they made to each other in the presence of Christ, remarriage may well be adultery.

21

Speaking in Tongues
1 Corinthians 12:4-11; 14:1-19

Now there are varieties of gifts, but the same
Spirit; and there are varieties of services, but the
same Lord; and there are varieties of activities,
but it is the same God who activates all of them
in everyone. To each is given the manifestation
of the Spirit for the common good.

1 Corinthians 12:4-7

WORDS FOR BIBLE TIMES

In Acts 2 we were introduced to the third person of the
Trinity, the Holy Spirit. While this was the same Spirit of
God already well-known to the Hebrews (1 Samuel 10:10; Job
27:3; Ezekiel 11:24), and the same Spirit who descended on
Jesus at his baptism (Mark 1:10-11), the outpouring on the
day of Pentecost was a spiritual baptism with new power and
presence. This was an encounter with God's Spirit that
marked a new day and a new order for planet earth. It was
nothing less than the inauguration of the Kingdom
announced and promised by Jesus.

In 1 Corinthians 12:4-11 and 14:1-19, we encounter the
fruits of this outpouring. Here are the gifts with which the Holy
Spirit infuses the church, so that the coming reign of God
might be embodied in the community of faith. The Greek word
for these spiritual gifts is *charismata* (singular, *charisma*), meaning something freely given. They are entirely a work of grace.
God bestows them however and on whomever God pleases.

We should note that the famous chapter on the gift of love (1 Corinthians 13) comes between the listing of *charismata* in 1 Corinthians 12 and the advice Paul gives in Chapter 14 about two of these gifts in particular. Just as the pouring out of the Holy Spirit at Pentecost had a purpose—to give the disciples the power and the gifts to witness to Jesus Christ "to the ends of the earth" (Acts 1:8)—so the gifts of the Holy Spirit have a purpose, namely, to build up the church.

The image of a body in which all the limbs and organs are interconnected and interdependent is a powerful reminder that God's *charismata* are never given merely for self-fulfillment (1 Corinthians 12:12-27; Romans 12:3-8). Their purpose is what today we might call "body-building."

Paul proceeds to give detailed attention first to the gift of prophecy. This gift was recognized in the early church as an inspired utterance, imparting not only knowledge and wisdom but an immediate discernment of Christ's will. It was not a *fore*telling of the future so much as a *forth*telling of the word of God. As Paul points out later in the letter, these "forthtellings" had to be tested by the church (1 Corinthians 14:27), not only because there was always the danger of false prophecy but also because the other spiritual gifts of the community were just as important in discerning the will of Christ.

The attention given to prophecy provides an introduction to Paul's major concern in this passage—the gift of speaking in tongues, or *glossolalia* (from the Greek *glossa*, meaning "tongue," and *lalein*, meaning "to speak"). The Corinthians had come to set high store by this gift, and Paul was the first to acknowledge its value as a mark of the Holy Spirit's presence. Indeed, he gave thanks to God for the frequency with which he was able to exercise this gift himself (14:18). Yet he warns the Corinthians that, as with all spiritual gifts, glossolalia is dependent on the other *charismata* of the church if it is to build up the body as a whole.

For one thing, glossolalia needs interpretation, without which it sounds like a musical instrument in the hands of someone who cannot play (14:7-9). For another thing, it can easily become a self-indulgent gift, providing much spiritual nurture to the person who exercises it but little to the rest of the body of Christ (14:13-17). Indeed, having thanked God that he himself has this *charisma*, Paul says that he would rather speak five intelligible words for the benefit of the church than ten thousand words in an unknown tongue (14:19).

WORDS FOR OUR TIME

While the spiritual gift of glossolalia has been present throughout the history of the church, we know it today primarily through the various Pentecostal denominations and through movements that are often described as "charismatic" or "neopentecostal" movements in traditional denominations.

One reaction to the manifestations of this gift of the Spirit has been to analyze it, psychologically and sociologically. But such analysis ultimately falls short of a satisfactory explanation, as do all attempts to rationalize the work of the Holy Spirit. Of course, we can gain insights into glossolalia by studying the human psyche, just as we gain insights into conversion by studying faith development. But such insights do not explain the spiritual source of God's *charismata*, nor do they indicate how we might use these gifts for the spiritual nurture of the church.

We might gain a better insight into glossolalia by looking at the history of the Pentecostal denominations that emerged from the Holiness Movement of the nineteenth century, predominantly in the United States. Many of the groups in this movement originated in the various churches of Methodism but found that their spiritual gifts, including speaking in tongues, were regarded with grave suspicion by the leadership of the church, especially by the clergy. The usual criticism leveled at these groups was that they claimed to be uniquely gifted with the Holy Spirit, thereby implying that other Christians were somehow spiritually inferior to them, an attitude regarded as arrogant.

While there may have been some grounds for this criticism, it was more than matched by the defensiveness of the established churches, which effectively drove these groups to form their own denominations around the beginning of the twentieth century. Generally the movement was known as Pentecostalism.

As a result of these separations, most church members in the traditional denominations today know very little about glossolalia and are somewhat uncomfortable with the subject. Many have never heard anyone speaking in tongues. They may have caught a snippet on the air from a television evangelist (for the most part, an extremely unreliable source). They may have heard descriptions from other witnesses. They may have a neighbor or friend who attends a Pentecostal church but are too polite to ask for an explanation or a demonstration (which is just as well, for people with this gift are not trained performers and cannot call it up at will).

The unfortunate fact of the matter is that the spiritual *charisma* of glossolalia is not a normative part of congregational life and mission in a great many of our churches. This renders all of us spiritually impoverished—those of us who belong to churches in which no one has the gift and those who belong to churches in which the gift is commonplace but is not shared with the church at large.

WORDS FOR MY LIFE

If you and I are to grasp the significance of Paul's advice to the Corinthians about their *charismata*, we must first acknowledge that the church is not like any other social grouping or institution. Congregations are called into being by Jesus Christ and are gifted and empowered by the Holy Spirit. That is why efforts to organize them along worldly lines will either fail or, much worse, will change them into something they were never meant to be. Christian congregations are more than human communities. They are the salt, light, leaven, and seed of the coming reign of God.

So, instead of asking whether your church is well organized, you should look among your sisters and brothers in Christ for the spiritual gifts that Paul lists in these verses and follow his advice in using them and sharing them. Rather than asking whether you have goals or programs or strategies, ask whether the *charismata* of your church are working together for the common good of the body of Christ.

Who are the wise people, spiritually speaking (1 Corinthians 12:8)? Who are the teachers (12:8)? Who are the ones whose faith is a constant source of strength to others (12:9)? Whose compassion and sympathy provide healing for everyone around them (12:9)? Whose quiet strength and perseverance always seem to move mountains miraculously (12:10)? Who can be relied on to speak boldly and prophetically when the church needs to hear the word of the Lord (12:10)? To whom does the church turn for discernment when it needs spiritual direction (12:10)? If some have the gift of glossolalia (12:10), are they recognized as a vital part of the congregation? And by no means least, what is your personal *charisma* as a member of the body of Christ?

If your church does not address questions such as these, perhaps you should ask, Why not? Maybe Christ is calling you to "prophesy . . . to other people for their upbuilding and encouragement and consolation" in the community of faith called the church (14:3).

22

The Christian Family
Ephesians 5:21–6:4

For no one ever hates his own body, but he nourishes and tenderly cares for it, just as Christ does for the church, because we are members of his body.

Ephesians 5:29

WORDS FOR BIBLE TIMES

When we recall 1 Corinthians 7:10-16, the words in Ephesians 5:21–6:4 seem to present a number of contradictions. Paul was at pains to convince the Corinthians of the equality of men and women, but here we find the father clearly at the head of the household. Paul assured the Corinthians that being unmarried was a worthy and even a preferable state, but here we find marriage extolled as the ideal way of life. Paul wrote to the Corinthians in clear expectancy of the coming reign of God, but here we find the family values of Greek and Jewish culture being affirmed the way they are. Readers of this letter are merely urged to regard them from a different perspective, as if the reign of God had already arrived in their midst.

All these contrasts seem to leave us with a lowered expectancy of a Christian household. The family arrangements we find here are hierarchical, and the respective roles and duties of the family members do not take the quantum leap forward in terms of mutual responsibility that we found in First Corinthians. We rather seem to have the reverse—the traditional family headed by the father but given the blessing of Christ's presence. Indeed, the relationship between the head of the house and the other family members is even likened to the relationship between Christ and the church.

The very power of this analogy is troublesome. Can any human father truly function in the same way as Christ? Are wives and children to regard their husbands and fathers as intermediaries between themselves and God? The problems of the analogy seem to multiply when we apply it to the reality of domestic life as we know it today, where few fathers behave with Christlike goodness and kindness and certainly do not do so with any consistency. Moreover, the misuse of this imagery across the centuries has subjected countless Christian women and children to masculine abuse and thereby made them gravely mistrust the gospel.

Why then is such imagery in the Bible at all, and how seriously should we take it? The answer lies in the context of this letter. It is generally agreed that Ephesians was written at a later date than most of Paul's letters and that in all probability it was meant to address a situation in the early church where domestic life was under severe pressure, even to the point of breaking down. The gospel was bound to cause such tensions because of the new freedoms that it brought to Christian households; parents and children could easily be set against each other as a result.

While these upheavals were initially accepted as preparation for the return of Christ and the reign of God he had promised, by the time this letter was written, the church already sensed that Christ's return was not as imminent as at first had been thought. So sustaining an active expectancy was increasingly difficult. Trying to live by some radically new house rules in a world that showed no sign of imminent change meant getting a second wind, so to speak, and establishing some criteria for a much longer period of waiting.

What better way to do this than to use the very image of Christ to impress upon church members that they should continue in well-tried customs unless they had a good reason to abandon them. If the world was not going to change as radically and as suddenly as had been thought, Christ would not expect them to surrender their traditional values all at once. In times of critical change there is always a fine line between freedom and license, and this letter urges the early church not to be self-indulgent. The teachings of Ephesians become problematic only if we turn their imagery into timeless axioms for family life.

WORDS FOR OUR TIME

We find similar pressures on family life in the late twentieth century, though for different reasons. Respect for the family is at a low ebb in our culture, not least because few families can survive today on one income. To make matters worse, we are manipulated by the mass media into seeking worldly wealth and possessions as a mark of social status and accomplishment. Even our children are economically manipulated.

Another pressure on family life today is the frequency of divorce and the number of single-parent families this produces. While a home with one parent can prove every bit as stable and nurturing for children as a two-parent home (and in some instances more so), all too often children and adults are scarred by destructive parental separations and disputes. William Styron's novel, *Sophie's Choice*, tells of a mother who, on arriving at a Nazi death camp, is confronted by a sadistic guard who makes her choose which one of her two children will die and which one will live. Seen from a child's perspective, this is not far removed from the choice that many divorcing parents ask their children to make.

This passage from Ephesians does not mean that families should return to a hierarchy in which the father has to serve as a Christlike head, but rather it has a message of mutual respect and interdependence. Keeping in mind that a head without a body cannot function and that a body without a head is lifeless, we can suggest a corollary to these verses: "Wives, love your husband as your own body; husbands, be subject to your wives, as to Christ. For Christ is present in both of you, to love and to cherish. Neither of you has a monopoly on the head or the body."

These verses also have an important word for daughters and sons: Honor your parents (Ephesians 6:1-2). In a culture where parents are increasingly being subjected to evaluation by their offspring, this might well be a difficult teaching for Christian children to accept. But parents in a Christian household are due honor, because there children first and foremost learn about Jesus Christ. The Christ-centered home will foster such honor, and the home that is not Christ-centered will be at the mercy of a culture that not only does not respect the family but is doing its best to destroy it.

WORDS FOR MY LIFE

Let us be clear that this passage cannot be used today as an argument that wives should be subject to their husbands any more than Jacob's marriage to Leah and Rachel (Genesis 29) can be used as an argument today for bigamy. The central teaching here is one of mutual care and respect, with Christ as the head of the house in and through the presence of the Holy Spirit. This relieves a Christian home of two impossible roles—a husband trying to measure up to Christ as head of the home and a wife who is denied the equality of personhood that the Holy Spirit has with Jesus.

Once again, we must be clear that the passage does not assign the role of instructor in the faith exclusively to the father (6:4). On the contrary, throughout Christian history mothers have often fulfilled this role more effectively than fathers. What the passage does ask is this: Have you, as a Christian father, done all you can to teach your children about Jesus Christ? And more, what example do you give them in the faith? If your children do not see you striving to be a faithful disciple, what does that tell them about their own discipleship?

The lesson is also clear for families: Whether it includes father or mother, whether it is a single-parent home or one blessed with both parents, the most important role of the Christian family is to teach one another about Jesus Christ, and especially to teach our children.

If our children do not see us reading the Bible, they will not take easily to reading it themselves. If they do not see us in prayer, they will not understand why they should pray. If they do not see us stand for God's justice in our daily lives, they will resent having to follow Christ's teachings in a world that always makes it difficult to do so. Nothing can make up for the lack of such formation in the Christian home.

23

Testing the Spirits
1 John 4:1-6

Beloved, do not believe every spirit, but test
the spirits to see whether they are from God;
for many false prophets have gone out into the
world.

1 John 4:1

WORDS FOR BIBLE TIMES

In the letters of John, as in the Fourth Gospel, we find the
early church confronting the first major challenge to its
teachings about Jesus Christ. The way the church addressed
this challenge, and the criteria it established for determining
the truth of the gospel teaching and authentic spiritual inspiration, have profound implications for the ministry and mission of the church today.

In 1 John 4:1-6, the question centers on the gift of
prophetic utterance—what today we might call "spirit-filled"
preaching or "inspired" teaching. Paul, while affirming
prophecy as a significant spiritual gift, ranked prophets subor-
dinate to apostles in order of authority (1 Corinthians 12:28).
This did not demean the gift of prophecy but established that
spiritual gifts *per se* did not necessarily define authentic Christian leadership. The ultimate authority lay with the apostles,
quite simply because they were the ones who had walked and
talked with Jesus and could verify his teachings. The opening
words of the letter state this authority: "We declare to you
what was from the beginning, what we have heard, what have
seen with our eyes, what we have looked at and touched with
our hands, concerning the word of life" (1 John 1:1).

In practice, of course, apostolic teaching without the inspiration of the Holy Spirit can quickly become a sterile traditionalism. But prophetic inspiration without the authority of apostolic teaching can quickly subvert the gospel with irrelevant or even faulty directives. Those who are gifted with inspired speech have a flair that is attractive to people who are hungry for spiritual guidance, and it is not always easy to determine whether they are inspired by the Spirit of Christ.

WORDS FOR OUR TIME

The criterion in this passage for the testing of the spirits may seem to be simplistic, but in fact it is profound and penetrating: Does the person who speaks with spiritual inspiration affirm Jesus Christ as fully human and fully divine? We need to press all aspects of this question as we "test the spirits" in our own time.

First, is the Jesus being proclaimed by an inspired preacher or teacher really human, or is he somehow presented as "superhuman" and therefore beyond our normal experience? Jesus of Nazareth was human just like us—eating Jewish food, celebrating at Jewish weddings, and playing with Jewish children. He also walked the dusty roads of Palestine, sweated Jewish sweat, and finally bled Jewish blood. If this is not the Jesus who is proclaimed, then however inspired a speaker might be, his or her spirit is that of an antichrist.

Second, is the Jesus being proclaimed truly the second person of the Trinity—God incarnate, the human being who was God? If Jesus is declared to be only a prophet, only a teacher, or worse, only a figure in the story of the church, then the Jesus being proclaimed is not the Christ. The power of the gospel lies in God the baby, God in human form, the God who came to share in the evil and the suffering and the sin of the world. Anything less than this and the spirit of the speaker, however inspired she or he might be, is likewise an antichrist.

Third, we must test the spirits of inspired preachers and teachers by asking whether they declare the implications of Jesus' humanity and divinity. The implications of his humanity are not only the exposing of our sin and our need to repent but also the need to follow his teachings as the rules of God's household. The implications of his divinity are that God has taken the initiative to invite us back home and is ready with all the grace that we need to follow these teachings in joyful obedience. However inspired they might be, preachers or teachers who proclaim a gospel without demands and make demands without the gospel speak with the spirit of an antichrist and are not to be trusted.

WORDS FOR MY LIFE

At this point, you might be wondering where all this is leading. Do I really have to "test the spirit" of every preacher who inspires me? Is it really necessary to run a check on every teacher who gives an interesting lesson to see whether she or he has a properly balanced doctrine of Jesus Christ? Am I obliged to brand anyone who fails this test an "antichrist"? What about people who hold different points of view? What about people who belong to different religious traditions? In fact, what about the love we are supposed to have toward everyone in the name of Jesus Christ? Calling them antichrists doesn't sound very loving.

These are valid questions, and they provide us with a helpful reminder that the Christian faith can never be a set of rigid beliefs. The freedom of the gospel will always require the church to be open to new directions from the Holy Spirit, and whenever the dogmas of the church have been separated from this spiritual freedom, Christians have become self-righteous and bigoted.

But whenever the spiritual freedom of the church has been separated from its apostolic teachings, Christians have become self-indulgent and careless about the gospel. The secret of faithful discipleship lies in obedience to the teachings of Jesus as the apostles related them to the early church and in obedience to the promptings of the Holy Spirit that inspire us to go beyond the teachings of Jesus in faithful service for the coming reign of God.

The problem being addressed in this passage is not whose beliefs are right and whose are wrong in the sight of God. The problem is rather a question of integrity. First of all, we should note that the writer of this letter does not condemn the many other religious beliefs of the time. The "false prophets" are criticized for another reason—claiming to be followers of Jesus Christ while not accepting the apostolic teaching of the church. The same criticism is made of the church at Laodicea in Revelation 3:15-16.

In other words, if you have received the gospel by grace through faith, then believe the gospel and live by it. If you have not accepted the gospel, then God must be withholding the grace you need to believe it, and you must therefore live according to whatever other faith God has given you. The worst thing you can do is to believe the gospel but then proceed to change it or ignore it to meet your needs or your preferences. That makes you an antichrist, inasmuch as you take the name of Jesus, but take it in vain. You would be far better off not to take it at all.

It was the lack of integrity of the false prophets that presented the early church with its gravest danger, and it presents you and me with the same danger today. Our task is to proclaim the gospel of salvation to a dying world. The mystery of our task is why so many people do not accept it as God's truth, but that is a mystery we must leave wholly in God's hands. What we must not do is change this gospel to make it more attractive to ourselves or to other people.

You and I must accept our responsibilities as Christian disciples by living out all the teachings of Jesus in the world, not picking and choosing which ones we will accept and which we will conveniently ignore. That is always the snare of the inspired preacher or church leader who is not concerned about right teaching. As John Wesley once said, such preachers offer people candy all the time; and the problem with candy is that it spoils the appetite for real food.

So we come back to the central teaching of these verses. Do you and I have to test the spirits of our religious leaders? Yes, indeed—for our own good and for the good of the church of Jesus Christ. By all means seek out inspired preachers and teachers, for without the Holy Spirit the word of God cannot be truly proclaimed. But at the same time, be sure they are inspired by the Holy Spirit and not the spirit of an antichrist. Only such discernment will truly keep the faith until the return of Christ and the coming of the reign of God.

Meet the Writers

Douglas E. Wingeier is Professor of Practical Theology and director of the Doctor of Ministry Program at Garrett-Evangelical Theological Seminary in Evanston, Illinois. He received his S.T.B. and Ph.D. from Boston University School of Theology.

Dr. Wingeier has served churches in Massachusetts and was minister of education and Wesley Foundation director at the University of Tulsa. He has been associated with Trinity Theological College in Singapore as professor, dean of students, and director of field education. He has also done teaching, research, and consultation in Haiti, Israel and the West Bank, Western Samoa, South Korea, and Central America. He has led travel seminars to Israel, the People's Republic of China, and Cuba and a work team to Nicaragua. He speaks fluent Chinese.

He has written extensively in the fields of theology, ministry, Christian education, and in United Methodist church school curriculum.

He and his wife, Carol, have four married children and six grandchildren.

David Lowes Watson is Professor of Theology and Congregational Life and Mission at Wesley Theological Seminary in Washington, DC. A native of England, he received his M.A. from Oxford University, M.Div. from Eden Theological Seminary in St. Louis, Missouri, and Ph.D. from Duke University in Durham, North Carolina.

Dr. Watson is an elder in the Southern Illinois Conference of The United Methodist Church and has served as pastor of rural and inner city churches. He has taught at Perkins School of Theology, Southern Methodist University and served as Executive Secretary for Covenant Discipleship at the General Board of Discipleship of The United Methodist Church. He is a past president of the Academy for Evangelism in Theological Education and also served on the board of directors of the Bicentennial Edition of *The Works of John Wesley*.

He has written six books and numerous articles in the fields of Methodist history and theology, evangelism, and congregational life.

He and his wife, Gayle, have a daughter and a son.